Dash Diet Cookbook for Beginners

An Easy-to-Follow Guide with Delicious Low Sodium Recipes and a 30-Day Meal Plan for a Sustainable Lifestyle

Table of Contents

Introduction

Do you have high blood pressure and don't want to go down the medication route? Sick of taking medication every day and hoping it will work? Finding a diet that helps lower your blood pressure, protects your heart and that's easy to follow and incorporate in your life has never been easy. Most so-called diets are nothing more than fads that are simply not sustainable and not easy to follow. That's where the DASH diet comes in.

This book will give you everything you need to help you lower your blood pressure naturally, with delicious, easy-to-prepare meals that the whole family will love. The DASH diet is scientifically proven to keep your heart healthy and reduce your blood pressure by limiting your consumption of unhealthy food, all while reducing your sodium intake. You'll find plenty of delicious, easy-to-prepare meals that will benefit your health without you really having to try.

Why You Should Read This Guide

It isn't always easy to start a new, healthier lifestyle. It isn't just finding the right diet for you. It's also about fitting it into your lifestyle, whether you have kids to worry about, a busy schedule, a vegan or vegetarian lifestyle, or anything else. The DASH diet takes the stress away, as it's easy to adapt to any lifestyle. This book provides simple advice to help you start your journey and sustain it over the long term.

Each chapter offers information on a separate aspect of the diet, giving you an overall view of the benefits DASH brings you. It is a simple guide, but you'll find plenty of other resources to help you. This guide aims to give you a kick in the right direction and set you on the right path for life.

It is written in easy-to-understand language, ensuring you understand the DASH diet and what it can do for you. There's a full month's sample eating plan, all the recipes to go with it, and plenty of practical tips to help you bring healthy eating into your life easily and as painlessly as possible.

Chapter 1: Introduction to the DASH Diet

Over a billion people have high blood pressure worldwide, and that number is set to rise every year. In the last 40 years, the number has doubled, and this is serious – high blood pressure is linked to many other serious conditions, including stroke, heart disease, some forms of cancer, and kidney failure, among others.

Diet plays an important role in controlling blood pressure, and the internet is full of so-called diets and strategies to bring high blood pressure down. Most of these are nothing more than fad diets that might work for a while, but they are not just unsustainable. They can also cause other serious health issues. The DASH diet is scientifically proven to reduce blood pressure, protect your heart, and improve your overall health.

1. The DASH diet is scientifically proven to improve overall health. Source: https://pixabay.com/photos/blueberries-milk-breakfast-fruit-1576409/

What Is the DASH Diet?

DASH stands for **D**ietary **A**pproaches to **S**top **H**ypertension, and it is a scientifically proven diet to help treat or prevent hypertension – high blood pressure – and lower heart disease risks.

The diet is focused on eating whole grains, lean meat, fresh fruit, and plenty of vegetables, and it was created when it was found that those who followed a vegan or vegetarian lifestyle had a much lower risk of high blood pressure. That's why there is a strong emphasis on veggies and fruits, with lean protein sources such as beans, fish, and lean poultry. What's missing from the diet is red meat, most sugar, bad fats, and salt.

Scientists believe this diet works for people with high blood pressure because it limits salt to no more than a teaspoon of sodium every day.

The DASH Diet Benefits

The DASH diet primarily aims to reduce or prevent high blood pressure but also has several other benefits. Here's how the DASH diet affects your body and health:

Reduces Blood Pressure: Blood pressure indicates the force placed on your organs and blood vessels by your blood passing through. There are two important numbers to take note of:

- **Systolic Pressure:** when your heart beats, this measures the pressure inside your blood vessels;

- **Diastolic Pressure:** the blood vessel pressure when your heart is resting between beats.

Normal adult blood pressure is less than 120 mmHg systolic and less than 80 mmHg diastolic and is normally indicated with systolic first, then diastolic, i.e., 120/80. If your blood pressure reads anything over these numbers, i.e., 140/90, then this is an indicator that you have high blood pressure, but the DASH diet has been shown to reduce blood pressure effectively.

Studies showed that those who followed the diet had lower blood pressure, whether they restricted their sodium consumption or lost weight. However, when they did restrict sodium consumption, blood pressure went even lower, and most studies show that people with the lowest salt intake had the lowest blood pressure. Perhaps the most impressive results were shown in those with high blood pressure, reducing their systolic pressure by 4 mmHg and diastolic by 5 mmHg. Those reductions were an average of 4 mmHg and 2 mmHg, respectively, in those with normal blood pressure who followed DASH. However, it is important to remember that reducing blood pressure does not automatically mean a decrease in the risk of heart disease, as many more factors can affect this.

It May Help You Lose Weight

While the DASH diet is not about losing weight, it is a benefit some people see. Most people with high blood pressure have been told they need to drop some pounds. It's been proven that, in most cases, overweight people are more at risk of high blood pressure and that losing weight can go some way towards lowering it.

However, the only way to lose weight on DASH is to reduce your calorie intake below what you burn off. The DASH diet, per se, is not calorie-controlled, as it emphasizes reducing sodium and eating a healthier diet overall. That said, if you are overweight, the DASH diet can help you lose weight initially because it removes processed, high-sugar, high-fat foods, and you are more likely to eat fewer calories overall.

However, it should not be followed strictly as a weight-loss diet.

Other Possible Benefits

The DASH diet may also offer a few other health benefits, such as:

- **May Decrease the Risk of Some Cancers:** some studies have shown that people on DASH lowered their risk of breast, colon, and other cancers.

- **Reduced Risk of Metabolic Syndrome:** some studies show that the risk of metabolic syndrome may be reduced by up to 81% when following a DASH lifestyle.

- **Lower Risk of Diabetes:** the DASH diet has also been shown to reduce the risk of diabetes, especially type 2, and can also boost insulin resistance.

- **Lower Risk of Heart Disease:** one study looked at women on DASH and found their risk of heart disease was 20% lower, while their stroke risk was reduced by 29%.

Most of the positive benefits come from the diet being high in vegetables and fruits, all shown to positively affect health and the body.

Is It for Everyone?

Many studies show that the DASH diet lowers blood pressure, especially when salt intake is significantly reduced. However, there are no clear-cut results to show that reducing salt will benefit everyone. Yes, you should reduce your sodium intake if you have high blood pressure. However, reducing sodium has fewer benefits if you are generally healthy and your blood pressure is normal.

What to Eat

There is no specific list of approved foods for the DASH diet. Instead, the focus is on eating specific servings of a wide range of food groups. In short, a balanced, healthy diet. How many servings you eat is dependent on your calorie intake, and the servings below are based on someone consuming a 2000-calorie-a-day diet:

6 to 8 Daily Servings of Whole Grains:

These include wholegrain or wholewheat bread and breakfast cereals, oatmeal, quinoa, bulgar, and brown rice.

1 serving could be:

- 1 ounce of wholegrain cereal, dry

- 1 slice of wholewheat or wholegrain bread

- ½ cup of cooked cereal, brown rice, or wholewheat pasta

4 to 5 Daily Servings of Vegetables:

No vegetables are off-limits on DASH.

1 serving could be:

- 1 cup of spinach, kale, or other leafy greens, raw

- ½ cup of raw or cooked sliced veggies, such as tomatoes, squash, broccoli, cauliflower, carrots, etc.

4 to 5 Daily Servings of Fruits:

Fruit is a given on DASH, and if you follow this lifestyle, you should expect to eat a lot of it. You can eat almost any fruit, including pears, apples, berries, peaches, mango, and pineapple.

1 serving could be:

- A medium apple or pear

- ½ cup of frozen, fresh, or canned peaches

- ¼ cup of dried apricots

2 to 3 Daily Servings of Dairy:

While the DASH diet does not exclude dairy, it does recommend low-fat dairy products, such as low-fat yogurt and cheese or skimmed milk.

1 serving could be:

- 1 cup of low-fat yogurt

- 1 cup of skimmed or other low-fat milk

- 1 ½ ounces of low-fat cheese

Up to 6 Daily Servings of Lean Meat, Chicken or Fish:

You should always aim for leaner meats and limit red meat to once a week or less.

1 serving could be:

- 1 egg
- 1 ounce of cooked fish, chicken, or meat

4 to 5 Weekly Servings of Seeds, Nuts, and Legumes:

This includes split peas, beans, lentils, sunflower seeds, pumpkin seeds, almonds, walnuts, peanuts, etc.

1 serving could be:

- 1/3 cup of nuts
- 2 tbsp of seeds
- 2 tbsp of nut butter
- ½ cup of legumes, cooked

2 to 3 Daily Servings of Fat and Oil:

Vegetable oil is recommended on DASH and includes canola, safflower, olive, and corn oil. Light salad dressings and low-fat mayonnaise are also recommended.

1 serving could be:

- 1 tsp of vegetable oil
- 1 tsp of soft margarine
- 1 tbsp of mayonnaise
- 2 tbsp of salad dressing

No More Than 5 Weekly Servings of Added Sugars:

While not completely prohibited, added sugar is minimized on DASH, so you need to look at how much table sugar, soda, and candy you consume. Alternative sugar sources)agave, maple syrup, honey, etc.) and unrefined sugars are also restricted.

1 serving could be:

- 1 tbsp of jam or jelly

- 1 tbsp of table sugar

- 1 cup of soda

DASHing Up Your Diet

The DASH diet doesn't have a set food list like most other diets do, so adapting the diet to your current lifestyle is pretty easy:

- Increase your fruit and veggie consumption.

- Eat whole grains instead of refined ones.

- Go for low-fat or fat-free dairy.

- Pick lean sources of protein.

- Use vegetable oils for cooking.

- Limit high-sugar foods, such as candy and soda.

- Limit foods with high saturated fat levels, such as full-fat dairy, fatty meat, palm oil, coconut oil, etc.

In terms of drinks, you can consume fresh, 100% natural fruit juices but in limited portions. Other than that, drink water, coffee, and tea.

Frequently Asked Questions

If the DASH lifestyle interests you and you want a natural way of reducing your blood pressure, you probably have questions you want answered. Some of the more commonly asked are:

Is Coffee Allowed?

There are no real guidelines, but if you are concerned that caffeine makes your blood pressure rise, avoid coffee altogether or drink decaf. It is known that caffeine can increase blood pressure, if only for a short while, especially if you already have hypertension. However, recent studies showed that coffee will not raise your chances of long-term risks of heart disease or high blood pressure, even if it causes short-term hypertension.

2.   You can still drink coffee even if you're DASH dieting. Source: https://pixabay.com/photos/coffee-coffee-cup-cup-drink-beans-2714970/

You can safely drink up to 4 cups of coffee daily if your blood pressure is normal. If you have high blood pressure, consider limiting yourself to no more than 2 days at most.

Is Exercise Necessary?

Exercise is an integral part of any healthy lifestyle, and studies have shown that, while the DASH diet is effective on its own, it is even more effective when combined with exercise. This shouldn't be surprising given the benefits of exercise on its own.

Some examples include:

- Walking briskly at a speed of 15 minutes per mile.

- Running at a speed of 10 minutes per mile.

- Cycling at a speed of 6 minutes per mile.

- Swimming laps for 20 minutes.

- 1 hour of housework.

What about Alcohol?

If you drink too much, your blood pressure will likely increase. Studies have shown that having more than three alcoholic units per day is linked to an increase in the risk of heart disease and hypertension. The DASH diet recommends that, if you must drink alcohol, do so sparingly and never go above the official guidelines of 1 or fewer drinks per day for women and 2 for men.

3. *Monitor your alcohol intake if you're DASH dieting. Source: https://pixabay.com/photos/glass-wine-drops-red-wine-drink-3077869/*

Who Is the Diet For?

The DASH diet is primarily for people with high blood pressure who need a healthy way of reducing it without resorting to fad diets and medication. It's also suitable for people who are overweight and at high risk of hypertension. Even though DASH is not a weight loss diet, it can result in some loss because it is focused on eating mostly fresh, whole fruits and vegetables, lean protein, and low-fat dairy while limiting sugar and salt intake.

The DASH diet is also one of the best for those looking to improve their health and reduce hypertension risks or blood pressure. That's because there is nothing complicated about it.

There are no specific food lists to follow, no hard and fast rules on what you must eat every day, and it isn't a fad diet. DASH is less of a diet and more of a lifestyle, focused on healthy food and simple recipes that anyone can prepare, and everyone can enjoy.

Chapter 2: Understanding Low Sodium Nutrition

The main focus of the DASH diet is to reduce salt or sodium in your diet to reduce hypertension. However, many people talk about salt and sodium as the same things. Table salt, which you add to your food, sometimes liberally, is known as sodium chloride, while sodium is a mineral component of salt. This chapter will discuss salt and sodium, its nutritional impact on your health, and how much you should eat daily.

4.   *The main focus of the DASH diet is to reduce sodium in your diet.*
Source: https://pixabay.com/photos/himalayan-salt-salt-seasoning-6624128/

Salt and Sodium

You've most likely heard that Americans are guilty of one thing – eating far too much salt. The human body requires sodium, but not as much as you think. High-sodium diets have long been linked with hypertension, which increases the risk of heart disease and stroke.

Regardless of what you might have been told or what you believe, more than 70% of dietary sodium comes from processed and prepackaged foods, not from what you add to your food when you cook and eat it. Many years ago, our diets consisted mostly of fresh whole foods, but today, we live on a diet of fast food, processed and prepackaged foods, white bread, canned foods high in salt and sugar, and sweets. Today, our food supply is full of sodium, and the only way to consume less is to change your diet. The USFDA is working hard to get the food industry to reduce sodium in many foods, and one of the easiest ways to ensure you eat less is to learn how to read the nutrition labels on your food.

Here's how:

- **Understand the Daily Value:** This refers to daily recommended amounts of nutrients. That figure for sodium is less than 2300 mg per day – just 1 teaspoon.

- **Understand and Use the % Daily Value:** This figure indicates the percentage of each nutrient's daily value in a food serving and shows how much it contributes to your diet daily. Use this to work out if your food serving is high or low in sodium, and make sure you choose foods that provide less than 100%. As a rule of thumb, if the label says 5% or less, this is low, while 20% or higher is considered too much.

- **Be Mindful of Serving Sizes:** The label indicates the nutrition per serving size, so be aware of what a serving size is so you know your sodium intake.

What You Eat Matters

The CDC (Centers for Disease Control and Prevention) estimates that around 40% of the sodium in a standard diet comes from certain foods:

- Burgers
- Burritos
- Deli meat sandwiches
- Egg dishes
- omelets
- Pasta mixed dishes
- Pizza
- Poultry
- Savory Snacks, such as popcorn, chips, crackers, etc
- Soups
- Tacos

However, you must remember that each food will have differing sodium levels, no matter how similar they are. For example, a typical burrito will have 2700 mg of sodium per serving, while a typical taco has 1540 mg. This is why you need to learn to read the nutritional label and compare foods before you buy them, not forgetting to look at the serving size.

5. *Certain food has more sodium than others. Source:*
https://pixabay.com/photos/burger-hamburger-bbq-food-
3442227/

Sodium in Your Food

Sodium has plenty of uses as a food ingredient. It is used in baking, curing meat, pickling vegetables, as a thickening agent, and as a flavor enhancer. However, many additives also include sodium and make a small contribution to how much is listed on the nutrition label. Those additives include sodium nitrite, baking soda (sodium bicarbonate), and sodium benzoate.

It might surprise you that even if a food doesn't taste salty, it can still have high sodium levels. This is why you cannot just rely on taste to test how much sodium is in it. For example, soy sauce, pickles, and other foods with high sodium levels typically taste salty, while pastries and cereals don't taste salty at all but are still high in sodium. Other foods you might consume liberally, like bread, can also add a lot of sodium to your diet, even though 1 serving may not be that high.

Here are some examples to give you an idea of sodium levels in your food:

- Jam sandwich vs. Vegemite sandwich: you would be forgiven for thinking the Vegemite was a whole heap higher in salt, but, in fact, the jam sandwich has just 30% less sodium. Why? Because the bulk of the sodium is in the bread, not the filling.

- Don't make the mistake of using garlic salt, celery salt, onion salt, or sea salt as so-called healthier substitutes – they still contain as much sodium.

- A small bag of chips and a bowl of cornflake cereal have roughly the same amount of sodium.

- There's more sodium in some sweet cookies than in savory ones.

- Choose Swiss, Mozzarella, cottage, or ricotta if you want a low-sodium cheese.

When you read the package labels, here's what you need to understand. Many manufacturers will make claims about sodium levels, which are often ambiguous. Here are some of the more common claims you might see and what they really mean:

The Claim	What It Really Means
Sodium/Salt-Free	It contains 5 mg or less sodium per serving.
Very Low Salt/Sodium	35 mg of sodium or less per serving.
Low Salt/Sodium	140 mg of sodium or less per serving.

Reduced Salt/Sodium	A minimum of 25% less salt than regular versions
Lightly Salted/Light Sodium	A minimum of 50% less salt than regular versions
Unsalted/No Added Salt/Sodium	No added salt during processing, but may not be free of salt or sodium unless explicitly stated.

The Effects of Too Much Sodium

Small amounts of sodium can help keep your body fluids balanced unless you are a profuse sweater, and it aids your nerves and muscles in running smoothly. The average amount eaten daily by most Americans is around 3400 mg, over the recommended amount.

Too much sodium can lead to several health complications, including:

- **Hypertension**

There is a strong link that is very well established between too much sodium and high blood pressure. In populations where the average sodium intake is higher than recommended, the levels of hypertension are much higher.

When you reduce your sodium consumption, you reduce your risk of hypertension and cardiovascular disease. However, it is important to note that other factors also play an important role: whether you exercise, your age, current blood pressure, weight, stress levels, and whether you drink alcohol (and how much.)

If you have hypertension, kidney disease, or diabetes or are overweight or older, too much sodium can have a negative effect,

Other Health Conditions

There is also evidence that too much sodium can lead to a higher risk of:

- Fluid retention

- Heart failure

- Hypertrophy of the left ventricular (thickening heart muscle)

- Kidney disease

- Kidney stones

- Osteoporosis

- Stomach cancer

- Stroke

Too much salt causes more calcium to be removed from your body via urine, which leads to an imbalance. If there is insufficient water in your body, it leads to high levels of sodium or hypernatremia, a serious condition occurring when sodium levels rise above 14 milliequivalents per liter in the blood. It's so serious that it can cause death, and one of the biggest symptoms is a very strong thirst, and this is usually treated by controlled water replacement.

6. *Consuming too much salt can be harmful to your health. Source: https://pixabay.com/photos/salt-salt-shaker-table-salt-3285024/*

As you can see, getting sodium levels right is a fine art, but if you can stick to the recommended one teaspoon or less per day, you won't go wrong. Just learn to read your food nutrition labels and make the right food choices.

Chapter 3: Getting Started with the DASH Diet

Getting started with the Dash diet isn't that difficult, but it will take some preparation. First, you need to set your goals and what you expect from your new lifestyle. Once you understand what you want, you can begin to draw up your eating plans and get your grocery list drawn up, which this chapter will focus on. Lastly, you will see two lists: the Dirty Dozen and the Clean Fifteen. As you will learn, this relates to food and pesticide residues.

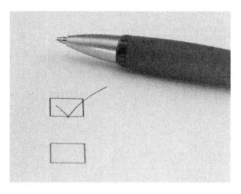

7. Draw up your eating plans and get your grocery list drawn up. Source: https://pixabay.com/photos/office-selection-write-paper-3199659/

Setting Your Goals and Expectations

One of the most common goals for any diet is weight loss, but that's not necessarily what the DASH diet is about. Sure, it can help you lose weight, but only if you follow a calorie-controlled version. For most people, the DASH diet is all about reducing their blood pressure and feeling better overall.

The best way to set your goals for DASH is to follow the SMART rules, as they seem to be the most successful for most people. However, one question many people ask is, why is there a need for goals in the first place?

Why Are Goals so Important?

Think about it this way. If you were heading out on a long road trip, would you just set off or use your GPS to get you to wherever you need to be? Going with the first option means you risk taking wrong turns and going in the wrong direction. Alternatively, if you take a little time to program your GPS first, you are more likely to get to where you want to be, even if you miss a turn. The same applies to diets and setting goals.

When you start a new, healthy journey, you need to set goals to help you succeed, and they must be specific. You could just say you want to lose 20 lbs. or reduce your blood pressure by 20 mmHg, but those are not specific goals. And when your goals are specific, you will find it much easier to recalculate them if you go off-plan somewhere along the way.

What Are SMART Goals?

8. *Make SMART goals. Source: https://pixabay.com/photos/goals-setting-office-work-note-2691265/*

SMART goals are among the most powerful because they give you a clear route ahead. SMART is an acronym, and each letter stands for a specific quality:

- **S**pecific

- **M**easurable

- **A**ttainable

- **R**elevant

- **T**imely

Let's look at these steps more closely in times of managing your hypertension:

- **Specific:** Instead of being vague and setting a goal of reducing your blood pressure, you need to be specific in how you will reduce these levels. The more specific your goals are, the better your chance of long-term success.

- **Measurable:** Your goals must be measurable to manage your condition successfully. Your doctor may have told you to monitor your readings at home or log your symptoms and readings. Those readings can help you measure your goals and ensure you are going in the right direction.

- **Attainable:** Instead of pie-in-the-sky dreams, ensure your goals are easy to achieve. While being a little ambitious can be a good motivator, it can also be your downfall if you take things too far. Be realistic and set goals you know you can achieve.

- **Relevant:** Your goals must be relevant to your overall aims and what you want to achieve over the long term. Relevant goals are an excellent motivator, give you a direction to follow, and focus on what you really want to achieve.

- **Timely:** Goals must have realistic deadlines. That way, you have something to work toward and a better chance of success.

How to Set SMART Goals for Hypertension

Here are a few examples of SMART goals to manage your hypertension:

Reduce Your Blood Pressure

"I want to reduce my blood pressure to normal levels within two months. I will do this by making healthy changes to my lifestyle, like getting more exercise and eating a better diet."

- **Specific:** this is a specific goal because you have determined that you want your blood pressure reduced to a normal healthy level.

- **Measurable:** your progress can be tracked by visiting your doctor regularly or by taking your own readings at home.

- **Attainable:** A deadline of two months is attainable with the right changes to your lifestyle.

- **Relevant:** Reducing your blood pressure and reducing your risk of other health conditions are critical to your health.

- **Timely:** You've given yourself a reasonable time of two months to achieve the goal.

That's your main goal. The next ones are all about how you achieve that main goal:

Take Regular Exercise

"I will do 30 minutes of exercise three times a week and track my progress by writing how long each exercise is and its intensity. Within three months, I will increase to five times a week."

- **Specific:** You will exercise for 30 minutes three times a week. It doesn't get more specific than that.

- **Measurable:** You can measure your progress by writing down how long you exercise and each session's intensity.

- **Attainable:** This is achievable if you stick to your goal of exercising three times a week.

- **Relevant:** Regular exercise has been proven to reduce blood pressure and make you feel better overall.

- **Timely:** Within the initial three months, you should have gotten yourself into a routine and be fit enough to add an extra two days a week to your plan.

Eat a Healthier Diet

"Within two months, I will increase my daily fruit and vegetable intake and limit how much processed food I eat. I will also switch sugary or milky drinks for water, herb tea, or black coffee."

- **Specific:** Your goal is to increase your fruit and vegetable intake and limit your processed food intake.

- **Measurable:** You can track your daily intake by recording what you eat.

- **Attainable:** You can achieve this because you are doing something towards it, i.e., limiting your processed foods, increasing healthy food intake, and replacing sugary sodas with water, tea, or coffee – no sugar!

- **Relevant:** It is entirely relevant because eating a healthier diet will benefit your health and wellbeing.

- **Timely:** It has an end date – two months – making it count.

Use Your Support System

"I will talk to my family and friends twice a week about how I struggle with high blood pressure. They will give me the support I need and help me stay motivated to meet my goals."

- **Specific:** Your goal states the specific thing you will do and how often you will do it.

- **Measurable:** You can monitor how often you communicate with your support system.

- **Attainable:** This is perfectly achievable so long as you make the effort.

- **Relevant:** This is highly relevant to people who struggle with hypertension because a support system is important to help you create and follow a healthier lifestyle.

- **Timely:** This is an ongoing goal.

Lower Your Stress Levels

"I want to have a plan to reduce my stress levels within six months. My plan will include more social interaction with friends and family, learning mindfulness, and being positive."

- **Specific:** This specifically states your intention to minimize your stress levels and how you want to do it.

- **Measurable:** Track your progress and ensure you are well on your way to getting your plan implemented or have started working towards lowering your stress levels.

- **Attainable:** Provided you have the right focus and are dedicated, you should be able to develop a workable plan.

- **Relevant:** Lowering your stress levels is crucial to living a healthy life and reducing your hypertension.

- **Timely:** You have six months to develop and implement your plan.

Limit Your Alcohol Intake

"I will reduce my intake to two drinks or less per week within three months. Reducing alcohol intake is important to keeping my blood pressure at a healthy level."

- **Specific:** Stating that you want to reduce your alcohol intake to no more than two drinks a week is specific.

- **Measurable:** How much you drink a week is easy enough to track.

- **Attainable:** Reducing your intake is easily doable, provided you are dedicated to doing so.

- **Relevant:** Cutting back on alcohol is critical to keeping your blood pressure at healthy levels.

- **Timely:** You have given yourself three months to reach your goal.

Take Your Medication as Your Doctor Prescribed:

"I will take my medication exactly as my doctor has prescribed and ensure my prescriptions are filled on time so I don't miss any. I will also use my phone to remind me when to take my medication."

- **Specific:** It is clear what you need to do – take your medication consistently and get your prescriptions filled on time.

- **Measurable:** You can easily monitor how much medication to take and when to take it.

- **Attainable:** If you stick to your prescribed schedule and take note of your phone reminders, this is perfectly achievable.

- **Relevant:** Your prescribed medication is critical for treating your hypertension and any other conditions it may have caused.

- **Timely:** There is no actual deadline, but this is an ongoing goal.

Quit Smoking/Vaping

"I will quit smoking/vaping completely within three months. I will make changes to my lifestyle, join a support group to help me, and ensure I have supportive friends and family around me."

- **Specific:** The goal is clear – you want to quit smoking/vaping.

- **Measurable:** Your healthcare provider could run regular carbon monoxide tests on you throughout the period.

- **Attainable:** This is an achievable timeframe unless you have a severe addiction to nicotine.

- **Relevant:** This is entirely relevant to your goal of having a healthier lifestyle, and it will definitely help lower your blood pressure.

- **Timely:** You have set a deadline of three months to be successful.

Identify Triggers and Avoid Them

"For the next two months, I will identify anything that triggers my high blood pressure and avoid them. I will record all changes and follow a healthy lifestyle every day to help reduce my hypertension risks."

- **Specific:** You have set a clear goal to identify your triggers and avoid them.

- **Measurable:** You will monitor your progress by recording any changes you note and any triggers you identify.

- **Attainable:** You can easily achieve this goal if you have a daily planned routine.

- **Relevant:** Identifying your triggers and avoiding them is critical to help you manage your hypertension.

- **Timely:** You have given yourself two months to accomplish your goal.

Get Sufficient Sleep

"I want to be able to sleep for a minimum of 7 hours every night within the next two weeks. I will have a plan for nighttime that helps me relax, such as reading for a while or writing my journal. I will set an alarm to ensure I have the same bedtime every night."

- **Specific:** You have stated a specific goal and how you will achieve it.

- **Measurable:** A sleep tracker on your phone could help you track your sleep.

- **Attainable:** If you stick to the same bedtime every night and use an alarm clock to remind you of bedtime, you can achieve this.

- **Relevant:** Good sleep is important to help you keep your health in good shape.

- **Timely:** You have given yourself a two-week deadline to achieve this.

Reduce Your Sodium Intake

"I will lower my sodium intake to below 2300 mg a day within five months. I will change my diet and make sure I understand nutrition labels to make sure I only buy low-sodium foods."

- **Specific:** You have a clear goal of what sodium intake to aim for.

- **Measurable:** You can track your progress by reading nutrition labels and noting what you eat.

- **Attainable:** Provided you make the right changes, you can easily achieve this within five months.

- **Relevant:** This goal is entirely relevant to helping you reduce hypertension, as too much salt is a big factor in causing it.

- **Timely:** You have a timescale of five months to achieve this.

When you write SMART goals, you have a better chance of succeeding in reducing your hypertension. Simple changes to your diet and lifestyle and using the SMART goal framework are the best ways of achieving this. Those goals are how you monitor your objectives over the short and long term, so make sure to take the time to write them properly.

Grocery Shopping Tips

Shopping is rarely anyone's favorite pastime, but there are ways to make it easier. If you are following a DASH lifestyle, there are some things you can do to make your next shopping trip a breeze:

- **Be Prepared:** Plan your meals for the week and make a list before you head to the store. That way, you can focus on what you really need and stop yourself from purchasing unhealthy options or things you don't need. Plus, it can save you money!

- **Do the Outer Aisles First:** Those are where the good foods are – the fruits and fresh veggies, dairy, whole grains, lean meat, and fish. Once you have what you need, you can head to the middle aisles for canned and frozen veggies, beans, fruits, and cereals.

- **Read Your Labels:** Even if you think food is healthy, you should always check the labels and compare foods to ensure you make the healthiest choices. Pick items with the lowest sodium, added sugars, and saturated fat per serving.

- **Explore the Fresh Produce Section:** Look for seasonal produce or for what's on sale to save money.

- **Eat First:** Shopping on an empty stomach is never a good idea, as it tends to lead to bad purchases.

- **Buy Foods Canned in Water, Not Oil:** This goes for meat, fish, and poultry. Make sure the labels also say there is no salt or at least low levels.

- **Buy Canned or Frozen to Save Food Waste:** This applies to fruits and vegetables, but make sure the cans are labeled as low sodium or have no added salt. Veggies should not be canned in sauce, salt, or any seasoning, only water. Before you cook canned beans or vegetables, drain and rinse them first to remove any salt. For canned fruits, buy those in water or natural juice or labeled with no added sugar. Frozen fruit should not have any added sugar, sweetener, or syrup.

- **Bread and Grains Should Primarily Be Wholegrain:** That means the first ingredient on the label should be wholegrain, not multi-grain or enriched flour.

- **Divvy up Your Snacks:** Divide them into individual portions in baggies or containers so you only grab what you need and don't eat more than you should. It's also a smart way to save money rather than buying individual snacks.

Making a Shopping List:

Here's a sample shopping list to help you get started on the DASH diet:

- **Fresh Fruit:** Choose seasonal fruits, like bananas, apples, oranges, melons, berries, and peaches, and get a good selection.

- **Fresh Vegetables:** Choose cooked and raw vegetables, such as carrots, broccoli, cauliflower, cabbage, peppers, spinach and tomatoes.

- **Whole Grains:** Choose whole wheat pasta, brown rice, whole grain bread, bulgar, whole grain oats, and quinoa to give your diet sufficient fiber.

- **Lean Protein Sources:** This means white meat, such as turkey and chicken without the skin, legumes, like lentils, beans, chickpeas, fish, and tofu.

- **Low-Fat Dairy:** Choose skimmed milk, low-fat cheese, and low-fat plain yogurt to provide you with calcium without the saturated fat.

- **Healthy Vegetable Oils:** This includes flaxseed, extra-virgin olive oil, and canola oil, all excellent sources of omega-3 fatty acids.

- **Seeds and Nuts:** Include a range of these in your diet, like chia and flax seeds, pumpkin and sunflower seeds, walnuts, almonds, etc.

- **Seasonings and Spices:** Include black pepper, turmeric, basil, oregano, garlic, and other similar herbs and spices.

- **Water:** You must drink at least 8 big glasses of water daily to keep your body hydrated.

Obviously, you should adapt this to your needs and preferences, keeping in mind that the DASH diet requires you to consume a balanced diet.

The Dirty Dozen and Clean Fifteen

How often have you been told to wash your fresh produce when you get home? There's a good reason for that – pesticides! A non-profit organization called EWG (the Environmental Working Group) produces a yearly list of the vegetables and fruits most and least likely to be contaminated with pesticide residues. Their research has shown that more than 75% of the fresh fruits and veggies purchased in the USA are contaminated, and the recommendations are to look for organic sources of these foods as much as possible.

The Dirty Dozen

This year's report identified a whopping 103 different pesticides on collard greens, kale, and mustard greens, while bell and hot peppers had 101. New additions this year are blueberries, with almost 80% of samples showing some contamination, and green beans, with over 70% of samples contaminated.

Here is this year's Dirty Dozen, in order:

1. Strawberries
2. Spinach
3. Kale, collard greens, and mustard greens
4. Peaches
5. Pears

6. Nectarines

7. Apples

8. Grapes

9. Bell peppers and hot peppers

10. Cherries

11. Blueberries

12. Green beans

These foods all had the highest levels of pesticide contamination from the 46 crops that were tested.

Using This List:

This is not a list of foods you should avoid eating. Instead, you should try to purchase organic options, although these still have some pesticides on them, which means they still need washing before you consume them. And that means a thorough wash, not just a quick pass under the tap. Perhaps a better way would be to learn how to grow your own vegetables and fruits and ensure you don't use pesticides or other chemicals.

The Clean Fifteen:

The EWG also produces a list of the fifteen cleanest fruits and veggies with the least residues. Avocado and sweetcorn were the best, with less than 2% of the tested crops contaminated. About 65% of all crops tested on this list showed no contamination at all.

This is the 2023 Clean Fifteen:

1. Avocados

2. Sweet corn

3. Pineapple

4. Onions

5. Papaya

6. Sweet peas (frozen)

7. Asparagus

8. Honeydew melon

9. Kiwi

10. Cabbage

11. Mushrooms

12. Cantaloupe

13. Sweet potatoes

14. Watermelon

15. Carrots

Be aware that the lists only contain rankings based on pesticide residues. They don't include bacteria, which can build up when the food is in the shop, being handled by untold numbers of people. Again, wash your food thoroughly before you eat it.

Chapter 4: 30-Day Meal Plan

One of the most important things you should do when you start a new diet is draw up your meal plan, if not for a month ahead, then at least every week. That way, you'll find it easier to stay on track and draw up your shopping lists every week. The 30-day meal plan is not set in stone. Use it to understand what kind of meals you can eat and as a basis to draw up your own plan. You can also swap meals around as you see fit, so long as you stay within the daily sodium limits. In the next chapter, you'll find all these recipes and more to help you draw up your weekly or monthly pans.

9.   Plan a 30-day meal plan. Source: https://pixabay.com/photos/planner-planning-plan-calendar-3485992/

30-Day Meal Plan

DAY ONE

- **Breakfast:** Banana Oatmeal Pancakes.
- **Lunch:** Tomato Garlic Lentil Bowls.
- **Dinner:** White Wine Garlic Chicken.

DAY TWO

- **Breakfast:** Quinoa Breakfast Bowl.
- **Lunch:** Vegetable Soup.
- **Dinner:** Shrimp Orzo with Feta.

DAY THREE

- **Breakfast:** Breakfast Sweet Potatoes.
- **Lunch:** California Sushi Rolls.
- **Dinner:** Chicken Cherry Lettuce Wraps.

DAY FOUR

- **Breakfast:** Banana and Brown Sugar Oatmeal.
- **Lunch:** Steak Salad with Blue Cheese and Strawberries.
- **Dinner:** Peanut Ginger Linguine.

DAY FIVE

- **Breakfast:** Raspberry Peach Puff Pancakes.
- **Lunch:** Turkey and Vegetable Barley Soup.
- **Dinner:** Black Bean Pasta.

DAY SIX

- **Breakfast:** Asparagus Omelet in a Tortilla Wrap.

- **Lunch:** Rice Bean and Corn Burritos.
- **Dinner:** Cabbage Roll Skillet.

DAY SEVEN

- **Breakfast:** Warn 'n' Fruity Breakfast Cereal.
- **Lunch:** Southwestern Vegetable Wraps.
- **Dinner:** Butternut Linguine.

DAY EIGHT

- **Breakfast:** High Protein Overnight Oats.
- **Lunch:** Black Bean and Sweet Potato Rice Bowls.
- **Dinner:** Pork Chops with Tomato Curry.

DAY NINE

- **Breakfast:** Scrambled Eggs with Spinach.
- **Lunch:** Shrimp and Nectarine Salad.
- **Dinner:** Thai Chicken Pasta Skillet.

DAY TEN

- **Breakfast:** Green Pineapple Smoothie.
- **Lunch:** Fish Tacos.
- **Dinner:** Sausage-Stuffed Zucchini.

DAY ELEVEN

- **Breakfast:** Berry Almond Smoothie Bowl.
- **Lunch:** Lentil Medley.
- **Dinner:** Peppered Sole.

DAY TWELVE

- **Breakfast:** Egg and Vegetable Scramble.
- **Lunch:** California Quinoa Bowl.
- **Dinner:** Citrus-Herb Pork Roast.

DAY THIRTEEN

- **Breakfast:** Overnight Quinoa Pudding.
- **Lunch:** Farro Salad with Roasted Vegetables.
- **Dinner:** Creamy Lemon Pasta with Shrimp.

DAY FOURTEEN

- **Breakfast:** Chocolate-Banana Protein Smoothie.
- **Lunch:** Tabbouleh Salad.
- **Dinner:** Slow-Cooker Vegetarian Bolognese.

DAY FIFTEEN

- **Breakfast:** Portobello Mushrooms Florentine.
- **Lunch:** Peppered Tuna Kabobs.
- **Dinner:** Roasted Salmon with Smoky Chickpeas and Greens.

DAY SIXTEEN

- **Breakfast:** Raspberry Yogurt Cereal Bowl.
- **Lunch:** Warm Rice and Pintos Salad.
- **Dinner:** Kedjenou Chicken.

DAY SEVENTEEN

- **Breakfast:** Strawberry-Blueberry-Banana Smoothie.
- **Lunch:** Asparagus Soup.

- **Dinner:** Salmon Cakes.

DAY EIGHTEEN

- **Breakfast:** Breakfast Salad with Egg and Salsa Verde Vinaigrette.
- **Lunch:** Sesame Chicken Veggie Wraps.
- **Dinner:** Sweet Potato Carbonara with Spinach and Mushrooms.

DAY NINETEEN

- **Breakfast:** White Bean and Avocado Toast.
- **Lunch:** Mixed Vegetable Salad with Lime Dressing.
- **Dinner:** Sheet-Pan Chili-Lime Salmon with Potatoes and Peppers.

DAY TWENTY

- **Breakfast:** Vegan Smoothie Bowl.
- **Lunch:** Shredded Pork Salad.
- **Dinner:** One-Pot Garlicky Shrimp and Spinach.

DAY TWENTY-ONE

- **Breakfast:** Peanut Butter-Banana Cinnamon Toast.
- **Lunch:** Quinoa Power Salad.
- **Dinner:** Sheet-Pan Chicken with Roasted Spring Vegetables and Lemon Vinaigrette.

DAY TWENTY-TWO

- **Breakfast:** Cantaloupe Smoothie.
- **Lunch:** Slow-Cooker Chicken and Chickpea Soup.
- **Dinner:** Eggplant Parmesan.

DAY TWENTY-THREE

- **Breakfast:** Open-Face Breakfast Sandwich.

- **Lunch:** Beef and Bean Sloppy Joes.

- **Dinner:** Seared Scallops with White Bean Ragu and Charred Lemon.

DAY TWENTY-FOUR

- **Breakfast:** Strawberry Basil Lime Smoothie.

- **Lunch:** No-Cook Black Bean Salad.

- **Dinner:** Salmon and Asparagus with Lemon-Garlic Butter Sauce.

DAY TWENTY-FIVE

- **Breakfast:** Spinach and Egg Scramble.

- **Lunch:** White Bean Soup.

- **Dinner:** Mexican Bake.

DAY TWENTY-SIX

- **Breakfast:** Tofu Scramble.

- **Lunch:** Slow-Cooker Pasta e Fagioli Soup.

- **Dinner:** Baked Halibut with Brussels Sprouts and Quinoa.

DAY TWENTY-SEVEN

- **Breakfast:** Quinoa and Veggie Collard Wraps.

- **Lunch:** Salmon Couscous Salad.

- **Dinner:** Pistachio-Crusted Chicken with Warm Barley Salad.

DAY TWENTY-EIGHT

- **Breakfast:** Mediterranean Egg Bites.

- **Lunch:** Mushroom-Swiss Turkey Burgers.

- **Dinner:** Beef Stir-Fry with Baby Bok Choy and Ginger.

DAY TWENTY-NINE

- **Breakfast:** Quinoa Bowl with Spinach and Strawberries.

- **Lunch:** Stuffed Sweet Potato with Hummus Dressing.

- **Dinner:** Grilled Salmon and Vegetables.

DAY THIRTY

- **Breakfast:** Mushroom Spinach Omelet.

- **Lunch:** Chipotle Chicken Quinoa Burrito Bowl.

- **Dinner:** Pan-Seared steak with Crispy Herbs and Escarole.

Tips

The DASH diet is an excellent diet to follow because it isn't as restrictive as many others. Sure, you have to cut your sodium, added sugar, and saturated fat intake, but as you can see from the meal plan above, you can prepare plenty of wonderful, delicious recipes without these ingredients.

It isn't always easy to go from a bad diet to a healthy one quickly, so if you struggle, follow these tips to help you get onto the DASH diet gradually. Before you know it, you'll be eating a healthy diet and enjoying it.

10. Get creative with your meals! Source: https://pixabay.com/photos/woman-cooking-vietnamese-cuisine-6754248/

- **Make Small Changes:** Don't impose strict eating habits on yourself. If you don't normally eat much fruit or veggies, gradually increase them in your diet.

- **Take It One Step at a Time:** You'll be more likely to stick to your new plan.

- **Check Those Food Labels:** When buying anything, look at the food labels and weed out the high-fat, high-sodium options.

- **Get Creative:** You know what you can eat, so get a little creative and work on recipes to help you stick to the plan.

- **Eat a Colorful Diet:** Make sure your plate contains a balance of all the right food groups, and if you want something sweet after dinner, have a piece of fruit.

- **Exercise Regularly:** The best results always come when you include exercise, so try to get 30 minutes a day a few days a week. If you are not used to exercise, start slowly and build up.

Chapter 5: Delicious Low-Sodium Recipes

Every diet revolves around creating delicious, healthy recipes that fit the guidelines. This chapter provides you with all the recipes mentioned in the 30-day plan and some extras to help you plan.

11. Low-sodium meals don't have to be boring! Source: https://pixabay.com/photos/fried-egg-breakfast-enjoy-the-meal-394171/

BREAKFAST

Banana Oatmeal Pancakes

Serves: 8

Ingredients:

- 2 cups of multigrain or wholegrain pancake mix
- 1 finely chopped firm banana
- ½ cup of steel cut or old-fashioned oats
- ¼ cup of roughly chopped walnuts

Optional Toppings:

- Extra sliced banana
- Mixed fresh berries

Instructions:

1. Follow the package instructions to prepare the pancake mix. Add the walnuts and chopped bananas and stir them in.

2. Coat a pan with cooking spray and heat until hot. Add ¼ cup of batter, cook until bubbles appear on top and flip. Cook the other side until golden brown.

3. Serve as is or with your choice of toppings.

Quinoa Breakfast Bowl

Serves: 1

Ingredients:

- ¾ cup of water
- ¼ cup of rinsed tri-color quinoa

- 2 tbsp of dried cranberries or goji berries
- ¼ cup of almond milk, unsweetened
- ¼ cup of unsweetened blueberries, frozen or fresh
- 1 banana
- 1 tbsp of pumpkin seeds
- 1 tbsp of almond slivers
- 1 tbsp of chopped walnuts
- 1 tbsp of organic maple syrup
- 1/8 tsp of ground cinnamon
- 1/8 tsp of vanilla extract
- Extra maple syrup and almond milk – OPTIONAL

Instructions:

1. Heat ½ cup of water to a boil in a small pan and add the quinoa. Turn the heat down, cover the pan, and simmer until the quinoa is cooked and the liquid is absorbed, about 12 to 15 minutes.

2. While the quinoa is soaking, place the berries in the remaining ¼ cup of water and soak them for 10 minutes. Drain and set aside.

3. Slice the banana in half widthwise. Slice one half and mash the other half using a fork.

4. Take the quinoa off the heat and use a fork to fluff it. Add the mashed banana, maple syrup, almond milk, vanilla, and cinnamon, and stir well. Transfer the quinoa to a breakfast bowl, and add the sliced banana, soaked berries, pumpkin seeds, almonds, walnuts, and

blueberries. Stir and serve warm with extra syrup and milk if desired.

Breakfast Sweet Potatoes

Serves: 4

Ingredients:

- 4 sweet potatoes, approx. 8 ounces each
- ½ cup of fat-free Greek yogurt, coconut flavor
- 1 chopped medium apple
- 2 tbsp of organic maple syrup
- ¼ cup of toasted coconut flakes, unsweetened

Instructions:

1. Preheat your oven to 400°F and line a baking tray with aluminum foil.

2. Place the potatoes on the tray and bake for 45 to 60 minutes or until soft. Alternatively, clean the potatoes, prick them with a fork, and microwave for about 12 to 14 minutes on HIGH, turning them once during cooking.

3. Slice a cross on the top of each potato, open it, and fluff the potato pulp with a fork.

4. Serve topped with yogurt, apple, and maple syrup and garnished with coconut flake.

Brown Sugar and Banana Oatmeal

Serves: 3

Ingredients:

- 2 cups of nonfat or skimmed milk
- 1 cup of quick-cook oats
- 1 sliced large banana
- 2 tsp of soft brown sugar
- 1 tsp of organic honey
- ½ tsp of ground cinnamon
- Extra milk or cinnamon – OPTIONAL

Instructions:

1. Bring the milk to a boil in a small pan and add the oats. Stir them in, reduce the heat to medium, and cook until the oats are thicker, about 1 to 2 minutes. Stir occasionally.

2. Transfer to a bowl, stir in the honey, cinnamon, sugar, and banana, and serve with extra cinnamon or milk if desired.

Raspberry Peach Puff Pancake

Serves: 4

Ingredients:

- 2 peeled, sliced medium peaches
- ½ cup of fresh raspberries
- 3 large whole eggs

- ½ cup of fat-free milk

- ½ cup of all-purpose flour

- ¼ cup of fat-free vanilla yogurt

- ½ tsp of sugar

- 1 tbsp of butter

- 1/8 tsp of salt

Instructions:

1. Preheat your oven to 400°F.

2. Place the peach slices in a bowl, add the sugar, and toss to coat. Stir the raspberries in gently.

3. Put the butter in a 9-inch pie tin, place it in the oven, and heat for 2 to 3 minutes or until melted.

4. In the meantime, lightly beat the eggs, then whisk in the salt and milk. Add the flour gradually, whisking it in.

5. Take the pie tin from the oven, swirl the butter around to coat the base and sides, and pour in the batter mixture.

6. Bake for 18 to 22 minutes until the pancake is brown and puffed up. Take it out of the oven and serve it with the yogurt and fruit.

Asparagus Omelet in a Tortilla Wrap

Serves: 1

Ingredients:

- 1 whole egg

- 2 egg whites

- 1 tbsp of fat-free milk

- 2 tsp of parmesan cheese, grated

- 1/8 tsp of ground black pepper

- 4 trimmed, sliced asparagus spears

- 1 chopped green onion

- 1 tsp of butter

- 1 warmed whole-wheat tortilla, 8-inch

Instructions:

1. Whisk the egg, egg whites, milk, cheese, and pepper in a bowl until thoroughly blended.

2. Heat a skillet over medium heat, coat with cooking spray, and cook the asparagus slices for 3 to 4 minutes, stirring occasionally, until tender but crisp. Remove the asparagus from the pan.

3. Heat the butter in the same pan and add the egg mixture. The edges should set straight away. As they set, move the cooked edges to the middle, allowing the uncooked eggs to flow out to the edges.

4. Add the asparagus and green onion on one half when the eggs thicken and are set through. Fold the other half over the top, cook for another minute, then serve wrapped in a warmed tortilla.

Warm 'n' Fruity Breakfast Cereal

Serves: 10

Ingredients:

- 2 cups of hot cereal, seven-grain version

- 1 peeled, chopped medium apple
- ¼ cup of chopped dried apricots
- ¼ cup of dried cranberries
- ¼ cup of raisins
- ¼ cup of chopped dates
- 1 tsp of ground cinnamon
- 5 cups of water
- ½ tsp of salt
- Chopped walnuts – OPTIONAL

Instructions:

1. Coat a large crockpot insert with cooking spray. Add the water, oats, fruit, cinnamon, and salt, stir to combine, and put the lid on. Cook on LOW for 6 to 7 hours until the cereal is tender and has thickened.

2. Serve hot topped with walnuts.

Overnight Oats with Chia Seeds

Serves: 1

Ingredients:

- ½ cup of rolled oats
- 1 scoop of protein powder – your choice (see below for options)
- 2 tbsp of low-fat Greek yogurt
- 1 tbsp of chia seeds
- 1 tsp of organic honey – OPTIONAL

- ¼ tsp of vanilla extract

Chocolate Chip:

- Chocolate protein powder
- 2 tbsp of sugar-free cacao nibs or chocolate chips

Blueberry Cheesecake:

- Vanilla protein powder
- ½ cup of fresh blueberries

Strawberry Shortcake:

- Strawberry protein powder
- ½ cup of chopped strawberries

Instructions:

1. You can keep the base recipe as it is if you don't want additional flavoring – it already tastes great.

2. Add the oats, protein powder, and chia seeds to a mason jar. Add the yogurt, honey, and vanilla extract, stir well, and cover the jar. Refrigerate overnight, and stir in the fruit or chocolate chips if using just before serving.

Scrambled Eggs with Spinach

Serves: 1

Ingredients:

- 3 whole eggs
- 3 ounces of baby spinach
- ½ tbsp of olive oil
- 1 ½ tbsp of skimmed milk

- Salt and pepper to taste

Instructions:

1. Heat the oil over medium heat in a frying pan.

2. Beat the eggs and whisk in the milk. Season to taste with salt and pepper.

3. Pour the mixture into the pan and scramble them, stirring constantly.

4. As the eggs begin to solidify, stir in the spinach and cook until it has wilted.

5. Serve hot.

Pineapple Green Smoothie

Serves: 1

Ingredients:

- ½ cup of almond milk, unsweetened
- 1/3 cup of plain Greek yogurt, nonfat
- 1 cup of baby spinach leaves
- 1 cup of banana slices, frozen
- ½ cup of pineapple chunks, frozen
- 1 tsp of chia seeds
- 1-2 tsp of organic honey or maple syrup

Instructions:

1. Place the yogurt and milk into a blender.

2. Add the banana, spinach, pineapple, honey, and chia seeds. Blitz to a smooth consistency and serve straight away, or chill for a couple of hours first.

Berry-Almond Smoothie Bowl

Servings: 1

Ingredients:

- ½ cup of sliced banana, frozen
- 2/3 cup of raspberries, frozen
- ½ cup of unsweetened, unflavored almond milk
- ¼ cup of fresh blueberries
- 5 tbsp of slivered almonds
- 1 tbsp of coconut flakes, unsweetened
- ¼ tsp of ground cinnamon
- 1/8 tsp of vanilla extract
- 1/8 tsp of ground cardamom

Instructions:

1. Place the milk, banana slices, raspberries, cardamom, cinnamon, and vanilla in a blender. Add 3 tbsp of almonds and blend to a smooth consistency.

2. Transfer to a bowl, add fresh blueberries and the rest of the almonds, and garnish with the coconut flakes.

Egg and Vegetable Scramble

Serves: 4

Ingredients:

- 12 ounces of thinly sliced baby new potatoes
- 4 cups of thinly sliced veggies of your choice – peppers, mushrooms, etc.

- 3 thinly sliced scallions, white and green bits divided
- 6 whole eggs OR 4 whole eggs and 4 egg whites
- 2 tbsp of olive oil
- 2 packed cups of dark leafy greens – baby kale, baby spinach, etc.
- 1 tsp of fresh herbs, minced – your choice
- ½ tsp of salt

Instructions:

1. Heat the oil over medium heat in a large nonstick or cast iron skillet.

2. Cook the potatoes, covered, for about 8 minutes until they begin to go soft. Stir frequently so they don't burn.

3. Add the white scallion parts and the sliced veggies. Cook for 8 to 10 minutes until the veggies are softening and turning brown. Add the fresh herbs, stir, and push the mixture to the edge of the pan.

4. Turn the heat down to medium-low. Beat the eggs and pour them into the pan. Add the green scallion parts and scramble them for about 2 minutes, stirring frequently.

5. Add the leafy greens, and take the pan off the heat. Stir to mix everything, stir in the salt and serve.

Overnight Quinoa Pudding

Serves: 1

Ingredients:

- 1 cup of quinoa cooked and cooled

- ¾ cup of unflavored kefir

- 1 tbsp of chia seeds + extra to serve

- 2 tbsp of organic honey or maple syrup

- 1 cup of fresh berries – your choice

- ¼ tsp of vanilla extract

- Pinch of ground cinnamon

Instructions:

1. Place the cooked quinoa in a bowl and stir in the chia seeds, kefir, maple syrup/honey, and vanilla. Add a dash of cinnamon, stir it in, cover, and refrigerate overnight.

2. Serve with fresh berries and extra chia if desired.

Chocolate Banana Protein Smoothie

Serves: 1

Ingredients:

- 1 whole frozen banana

- ½ cup of nonfat milk

- ½ cup of red lentils, cooked

- 1 tsp of organic maple syrup

- 2 tbsp of cocoa powder, unsweetened

Instructions:

1. Place the banana in a blender, add the cooked lentils, milk, syrup, and cocoa, and blend to a smooth puree.

2. Serve straight away, or chill it first.

Portobello Mushrooms Florentine

Serves: 2

Ingredients:

- 2 large, destemmed portobello mushrooms
- 1 chopped small onion
- 1 cup of baby spinach leaves
- 2 whole eggs
- ¼ cup of feta or goat cheese, crumbled
- ½ tsp of olive oil
- 1/8 tsp of pepper
- 1/8 tsp of salt
- 1/8 tsp of garlic salt
- Fresh basil, minced – OPTIONAL

Instructions:

1. Preheat your oven to 425°F.

2. Spray cooking spray over the mushrooms and place them in a large pan, stem-side up. Season with salt, pepper, and garlic salt, and bake for about 10 minutes until tender.

3. Meanwhile, heat a little oil in a nonstick frying pan and sauté the onion for a couple of minutes, until tender.

4. Add the spinach and cook until wilted.

5. Whisk the eggs, add the salt, and pour them into the skillet. Cook, stirring frequently, until the eggs have thickened and are set.

6. Serve the mushrooms with the eggs spooned on top and garnished with crumbled cheese and fresh basil.

Raspberry Yogurt Cereal Bowl

Serves: 1

Ingredients:

- 1 cup of plain, nonfat yogurt
- ½ cup of shredded wheat cereal, minis
- ¼ cup of fresh raspberries
- 1 tsp of pumpkin seeds
- 2 tsp of mini semi-sweet chocolate chips
- ¼ tsp of ground cinnamon

Instructions:

1. Put the yogurt in a bowl.
2. Add the shredded wheat, chocolate chips, raspberries, and pumpkin seeds, and garnish with the cinnamon.

Strawberry, Banana, Blueberry Smoothie

Serves: 1

Ingredients:

- ½ cup of frozen blueberries
- ½ cup of frozen strawberries
- 1 small banana
- ¾ cup of unsweetened cashew milk, chilled
- 1 tbsp of hulled hemp seeds

- 1 tbsp of cashew butter

Instructions:

1. Pour the milk into a blender and add the strawberries, banana, blueberries, butter, and hemp seeds.

2. Blend to a smooth puree. If necessary, add a little more milk until you reach the consistency you want.

3. Serve straight away.

Breakfast Salad with Egg and Salsa Verde Vinaigrette

Serves: 1

Ingredients:

- 3 tbsp of low-sodium, low-sugar salsa Verde
- ½ cup of rinsed, drained red kidney beans
- ¼ sliced avocado
- 1 whole egg
- 1 tbsp + 1 tsp of olive oil
- 2 cups of salad greens
- 2 tbsp of chopped fresh cilantro + extra for garnish
- 8 tortilla chips, blue corn

Instructions:

1. Put the salsa in a bowl with 2 tbsp cilantro and 1 tbsp olive oil. Whisk together.

2. Place the salad greens in a shallow bowl and add half the dressing. Toss to combine, and add layers of beans, chips, and avocado slices on top.

---

3. Heat the rest of the oil over medium-high heat and fry the egg for about 2 minutes. The yolk should be slightly runny, but the white should be completely cooked.

4. Serve the salad with the egg on top and the rest of the salad dressing. Garnish with extra cilantro.

White Bean and Avocado Toast

Serves: 1

Ingredients:

- 1 slice of toasted whole-wheat bread
- ½ cup of rinsed, drained white beans
- ¼ mashed avocado
- Salt and pepper
- A pinch of crushed red pepper flakes

Instructions:

1. Spread the mashed avocado over the toast.

2. Top with white beans and season to taste with salt, pepper, and red pepper flakes.

Vegan Smoothie Bowl

Serves: 1

Ingredients:

- 1 cup of mixed frozen berries
- 1 large banana
- ½ cup of non-dairy milk, unsweetened
- ¼ cup of unsweetened pineapple chunks

- ½ sliced kiwi
- 1 tbsp of almond slivers
- 1 tbsp of coconut flakes, unsweetened
- 1 tsp of chia seeds

Instructions:

1. Place the berries, milk, and banana in a blender and process to a smooth consistency.
2. Transfer it to a bowl and add kiwi, pineapple, coconut, almonds, and chia seeds. Stir and serve.

Peanut Butter-Banana Cinnamon Toast

Serves: 1

Ingredients:

- 1 slice of toasted whole-wheat bread
- 1 tbsp of low-salt, low-sugar peanut butter
- 1 sliced small banana
- Cinnamon

Instructions:

1. Spread the peanut butter over the toast.
2. Top with slices of banana, and add a little ground cinnamon to taste.

Cantaloupe Smoothie

Serves: 1

Ingredients:

- 1 ripe banana, frozen with the peel on

- 2 cups of ripe cantaloupe, chopped
- ½ cup of low-fat/nonfat plain yogurt
- 2 tbsp of skimmed or nonfat milk powder
- 1 ½ tbsp of orange juice concentrate, frozen
- ½ tsp of vanilla extract

Instructions:

1. Let the banana thaw until the skin starts to go soft – this will take about 2 minutes.
2. Use a sharp paring knife to remove the skin and chop the banana into small chunks.
3. Place the banana in a blender, add the cantaloupe, milk powder, yogurt, vanilla, and juice concentrate, and blend to a smooth consistency.
4. Serve immediately.

Open Face Breakfast Sandwich

Serves: 4

Ingredients:

- 4 slices whole wheat bread
- ¼ cup of shredded fresh Parmigiano-Reggiano cheese
- ¾ cup of ricotta cheese, part-skim
- 4 whole eggs
- 2 cups of arugula
- 1 tbsp of olive oil
- 1 ½ tsp of lemon juice

- ½ tsp of salt
- ½ tsp of black pepper
- 1 tsp of fresh thyme, chopped
- Cooking spray

Instructions:

1. Spray both sides of each slice of bread with cooking spray. Grill or toast it until golden brown.

2. Place the arugula in a bowl with the 2 tsp olive oil, lemon juice, ¼ tsp pepper, and 1/8 tsp salt. Toss to combine.

3. Heat 1 tsp olive oil over medium heat and cook the eggs for 2 minutes. Cover the pan, cook for 1 minute, or until the whites are set, and remove the pan from the heat.

4. Combine the Parmigiano-Reggiano, ricotta, thyme, and ¼ tsp of salt in a bowl.

5. Spread the cheese mixture evenly over the bread, add the arugula mixture, and top with an egg. Season with salt and pepper and serve straight away.

Strawberry Basil Lime Smoothie

Serves: 1

Ingredients:

- 1 ½ cups of frozen strawberries
- 1 can of coconut milk
- 2 tbsp of organic maple syrup
- 2 tsp of fresh lime juice

- 10 fresh whole basil leaves

Instructions:

1. Place the coconut milk in a blender, add the strawberries, maple syrup, lime juice, and basil leaves, and blend to a smooth puree.

2. Serve over ice, as is, or chill it first.

Tofu Scramble

Serves: 2

Ingredients:

- 1 lb. of extra-firm tofu
- 15 ounces of rinsed, drained black beans
- 1 onion
- 3 garlic cloves
- 2 to 3 Roma tomatoes
- ½ cup of destemmed, chopped fresh cilantro
- ¼ cup of nutritional yeast
- 1 tsp of smoked paprika
- 1 tsp of ground cumin
- ¼ tsp of ground turmeric
- Salt

Optional Toppings:

- Salsa
- Sliced avocado
- Pico de Gallo

- Hot sauce

Instructions:

1. Place the tofu on paper towels, weigh it down, and drain the excess liquid.

2. Heat a little oil over medium heat in a large pan. Add the onion and a pinch of salt, and cook for 7 to 8 minutes.

3. Dice the tomatoes and crumble the drained tofu.

4. Add the garlic to the onion, cook for half a minute, then add the tomato and tofu. Stir well, and cook for 10 minutes, stirring now and then.

5. Put the turmeric, cumin, and paprika in a small bowl and whisk gently to combine. Stir in 1 to 2 tbsp of water until you have a smooth paste.

6. Stir the mixture into the pan, add the nutritional yeast, and stir.

7. Add half the beans and continue adding until you have the desired amount.

8. Add the cilantro, stir, and cook for about 3 minutes until the beans are hot all the way through.

9. Serve hot with toppings of your choice.

Quinoa and Veggie Collard Wraps

Serves: 4

Ingredients:

- 4 whole collard leaves
- ½ cup of hummus

- 1 cup of quinoa, cooked

- 1 medium tomato

- 1 medium cucumber

- 2 grated carrots

- 1 sliced avocado

- ½ cup of sprouts

Instructions:

1. Add an inch of water to a large skillet and bring it to a boil. Drop one collard leaf into the water, submerge it, and cook it for 15 to 20 seconds until bright green all over and cooked. Remove and set aside, then repeat with the other three leaves. Let them cool off completely.

2. When the leaves are cool, slice the stem out carefully. To do this, run a sharp knife from near the top of the leaf down the rib, but do not damage the leaf in any way or separate it. Remove the stem and discard.

3. Spread the hummus over each leaf, and top with cooked quinoa, tomato, carrot, avocado, and sprouts.

4. Starting from the side facing you, fold each leaf over the filling, rolling it as tight as you can.

5. Serve or store for up to 3 days in the refrigerator.

Mediterranean Egg Bites

Serves: 12 bites

Ingredients:

- 6 eggs

- 6 egg whites
- ¼ cup of skimmed, nonfat, or non-dairy milk
- ¼ cup of diced red onion
- ¼ cup of diced sundried tomatoes
- 2 ounces of low-fat feta
- 2 cups of fresh spinach leaves
- ½ tsp of fresh dill
- ½ tsp of garlic powder
- ¼ tsp of lemon pepper – OPTIONAL
- Salt and pepper

Instructions:

1. Preheat your oven to 350°F and grease a 12-cup muffin tin lightly.

2. Crack the eggs into a bowl, add the egg whites and milk, and whisk.

3. Add the feta, spinach, tomatoes, and onions, stir, and season with salt and pepper, dill, garlic powder, and lemon pepper if using, and stir well.

4. Pour the mixture into the muffin cups, filling them about ¾ full.

5. Bake for about 20 minutes. Insert a toothpick in the center of an egg bite. If it comes out clean, the muffins are cooked. If not, cook in two-minute increments until they are.

6. Remove from the oven, leave to cool, and store in the refrigerator.

Quinoa Bowl with Spinach and Strawberries

Serves: 2

Ingredients:

- ½ cup of dry quinoa
- 1 peeled, seeded mango, sliced thinly
- 1 peeled, seeded avocado, sliced thinly
- 4 large strawberries OR 8 small, sliced thinly
- ¼ red onion, sliced thinly
- 4 cups of washed, dried baby spinach leaves
- ¼ cup of crumbled feta cheese
- 2 tbsp of fresh, chopped cilantro
- ½ lime, thinly sliced

For the Dressing:

- ¼ cup of olive oil
- ¼ cup of lemon juice
- 2 tsp of organic honey
- 1 tsp of poppy seeds
- ¼ tsp of sea salt
- ¼ tsp of black pepper

Instructions:

1. Bring a cup of water to a boil and cook the quinoa as per the package directions. Spread it to cool on a baking tray.

2. Make the dressing by combining the olive oil, lemon juice, poppy seeds, honey, and salt and pepper in a small jar and shaking well to mix.

3. Divide the spinach between two salad bowls and top with the quinoa, mango, avocado, strawberries, onion, and cheese.

4. Drizzle with dressing and garnish with cilantro and lime slices.

Mushroom Spinach Omelet

Serves: 1

Ingredients:

- 5 sliced baby Bella mushrooms
- 1 tbsp of olive oil
- 1 ½ cups of fresh spinach leaves
- ¼ cup of red onion, sliced
- 1 ounce of goat cheese
- 1 egg
- 2 egg whites
- Cooking spray
- Diced scallions for garnish

Instructions:

1. Heat a skillet over medium-high heat and add the oil. Cook the onions for 2 to 3 minutes until they are translucent, stirring occasionally.

2. Add the mushrooms and cook for 4 to 5 minutes until lightly browned.

3. Add the spinach and cook for about 2 minutes until the leaves have wilted. Season with salt and pepper, remove from the heat and set aside.

4. Heat another skillet over medium heat and add cooking spray.

5. Whisk the egg and egg whites together and pour it into the skillet. Leave it for a minute before you gently lift the edges and tilt the pan to let the uncooked egg run underneath the cooked edges. Continue until the eggs are set and no longer runny.

6. Spoon the mushrooms onto one half of the omelet and add the crumbled cheese. Fold the other half of the omelet over the top, cook it for another half a minute, then serve garnished with green onions.

Spinach and Egg Scramble with Raspberries

Serves: 1

Ingredients:

- 1 ½ cups of baby spinach leaves
- 2 whole eggs
- 1 slice of toasted wholegrain bread
- 1 tsp of canola oil
- ½ cup of fresh raspberries
- Salt and pepper to taste

Instructions:

1. Heat a small skillet over medium-high and add the oil. When the oil is hot, add the spinach and cook for a couple of minutes until wilted, stirring frequently.

2. Lift the spinach onto a plate, use a clean paper towel to wipe out the skillet, and heat again over medium heat.

3. Beat the eggs and pour into the hot pan, stirring occasionally, until set and cooked through. Add the spinach, season with salt and pepper, and stir to combine.

4. Serve on the toast with a side of raspberries.

LUNCH

Tomato-Garlic Lentil Bowls

Serves: 6

Ingredients:

- 2 chopped medium onions
- 4 minced garlic cloves
- 2 cups of rinsed dry brown lentils
- 1 tbsp of olive oil
- 1 tsp of salt
- ½ tsp of paprika
- ½ tsp of ground ginger

- ½ tsp of pepper

- 3 cups water

- 3 tbsp of tomato paste

- ¼ cup of lemon juice

- ¾ cup of nonfat plain Greek yogurt

- Chopped fresh or tinned tomatoes and cilantro – OPTIONAL

Instructions:

1. Heat the oil in a large soup pot over medium-high heat, and cook the onions until translucent, about 2 minutes. Add the garlic and cook for another minute.

2. Add the lentils, water, salt, pepper, paprika, and ginger, stir well and bring it to a boil. Turn the heat down, cover the pot, and simmer for about 25 to 30 minutes until the lentils are tender.

3. Add the tomato paste and lemon juice, stir, and cook until heated through. Stir in the chopped tomatoes if using, and serve with yogurt and cilantro.

Hearty Vegetable Soup

Serves: 16 (4 quarts)

Ingredients:

- 1 tbsp of olive oil

- 8 sliced medium carrots

- 2 chopped large onions

- 4 chopped celery stalks

- 1 seeded and chopped large green pepper

- 4 cups of water
- 1 can of diced tomatoes with juices (28 ounces)
- 2 cups of V8 juice
- 2 cups of chopped green cabbage
- 2 cups of frozen green beans
- 2 cups of frozen garden peas
- 1 cup of frozen corn
- 1 can of rinsed, drained chickpeas or garbanzo beans (15 ounces)
- 1 garlic clove
- 1 whole bay leaf
- 2 tsp of chicken or vegetable bouillon granules
- 1 ½ tsp of dried parsley
- 1 tsp of dried marjoram
- 1 tsp of dried thyme
- 1 tsp of salt
- ½ tsp of dried basil
- ¼ tsp of pepper

Instructions:

1. Heat the oil in a medium soup pot over medium-high heat.

2. Add the carrots, celery, onion, and green pepper and sauté them for a few minutes until crisp-tender.

3. Add the garlic and cook for a minute, stirring frequently.

4. Add all the other ingredients, stir, and bring to a boil.

5. Turn the heat down, cover the pan, and simmer for 1 to 1 ½ hours until the vegetables are tender but not mushy. Lift the bay leaf out and serve immediately.

6. Leftovers can be refrigerated or frozen.

California Sushi Rolls

Serves: 64 pieces

Ingredients:

- 2 cups of rinsed and drained sushi rice
- 2 cups of water
- ¼ cup of rice wine vinegar
- 2 tbsp of sugar
- 2 tbsp of toasted sesame seeds
- 2 tbsp of black sesame seeds
- 8 nori sheets
- 1 small cucumber, seeded and sliced into matchsticks
- 3 ounces of imitation crabmeat, sliced into matchsticks
- 1 ripe avocado, peeled, seeded, and sliced into matchsticks
- ½ tsp of salt
- Bamboo sushi mat

Optional Ingredients:

- Prepared wasabi
- Low-salt soy sauce

- Pickled ginger slices

Instructions:

1. Add the rice and water to a large saucepan, stir, and leave it for 30 minutes. Then, bring it to a boil over medium-high heat.

2. Turn the heat down to low, put the lid on, and simmer for 15 to 20 minutes until the rice is tender and the water has all been absorbed. Take the pan off the heat and leave it to one side to cool down with the lid on.

3. Mix the sugar, vinegar, and salt in a small bowl, stirring to dissolve the salt and sugar.

4. Place the cooled rice in a shallow bowl and drizzle the vinegar mix over it. Use a wooden spoon to slice through it, mixing the rice and cooling it a little more. Place a damp, clean cloth over the bowl to keep it moist. You can make this up to 2 hours before you need it, but do not refrigerate it – just leave it standing with a damp cloth over it.

5. Mix the sesame seeds on a plate and set them aside. Lay the bamboo sushi mat on a firm surface so the mat rolls away from you. Place a sheet of plastic wrap over it and drop ¾ cup of the rice on it.

6. Wet your fingers a bit and press the rice to form an 8 x 8-inch even, flat square. Place a nori sheet on top.

7. Place a little crabmeat, cucumber, and avocado on the sheet, about 1 ½ inches from the bottom edge. Roll the rice up over it, dropping the plastic wrap as you go, and compress the mixture into a tight roll.

8. Remove the mat and roll the entire roll in the sesame seeds. Wrap it in plastic wrap and repeat with the rest of the ingredients, making 8 rolls.

9. Slice each roll into 8 even-sized rolls and serve with the wasabi, ginger, and soy sauce for dipping.

Steak Salad with Blue Cheese and Strawberries

Serves: 4

Ingredients:

- 1 lb. of top sirloin steak, about ¾-inch thick
- 2 tbsp of lime juice
- 2 tsp of olive oil
- ½ tsp of salt
- ¼ tsp of pepper

For the Salad:

- 10 cups of torn romaine leaves
- 2 cups of halved strawberries
- ¼ cup of red onion, thinly sliced
- ¼ cup of blue cheese, crumbled
- ¼ cup of chopped, toasted walnuts
- Low-fat balsamic vinaigrette

Instructions:

1. Lay the steak out and season it generously with salt and pepper. Set aside.

---

2. Heat the olive oil in a large skillet over medium heat. When hot, cook the steak for 5 to 7 minutes on each side or until cooked to your requirements. As a rule, if you want medium-rare, it should be 135°F inside, while medium should be 140°F and medium-well should be 145°F.

3. Lift the steak from the pan and leave it on a plate for 5 minutes. Slice it into thin strips and toss it in the lime juice.

4. Arrange the romaine lettuce on a plate and top with the onion and strawberries. Layer the steak slices on top, add the toasted walnuts and cheese, and serve drizzled with the vinaigrette.

Tip:

If you want a lower-calorie meal, omit the cheese and walnuts, as they add approximately 40 calories to each serving.

Turkey and Vegetable Barley Soup

Serves: 6 (2 quarts)

Ingredients:

- 6 cups of low-salt chicken broth
- 5 chopped medium carrots
- 1 chopped medium onion
- 2 cups of cooked turkey breast, cubed
- 2 cups of fresh baby spinach leaves
- 2/3 cup of quick-cook barley
- 1 tsp of canola oil

- ½ tsp of pepper

Instructions:

1. Heat the oil in a large pan over medium-high heat.

2. Cook the onions and carrots for 4 to 5 minutes, stirring occasionally, until the carrots are tender but crisp.

3. Add the broth and barley, stir, and bring it to a boil. Turn the heat down, put the lid on, and simmer for about 10 to 15 minutes until the barley and carrots are tender.

4. Add the spinach and turkey, season with the pepper, stir, and cook until the turkey is hot.

5. Serve immediately.

6. Leftovers may be refrigerated or frozen.

Rice, Corn and Bean Burritos

Serves: 8

Ingredients:

- 1 can of rinsed, drained black beans (15 ounces)

- 1 ½ cups of cooked brown rice

- 1 1/3 cups of frozen or fresh corn kernels

- 1 chopped medium onion

- 1 sliced medium green bell pepper

- 2 minced garlic cloves

- 1 tbsp of canola oil

- 1 ½ tsp of chili powder

- ½ tsp of ground cumin

- ¾ cup of low-fat cheddar cheese, shredded

- ½ cup of low-fat plain yogurt

- 2 sliced scallions

- ½ cup of salsa

- 8 whole wheat flour tortillas (8-inch diameter)

Ingredients:

1. Heat the oil in a large skillet over medium-high heat.

2. Cook the pepper, corn, and onions and cook for a few minutes, until tender, stirring occasionally.

3. Add the chili powder, garlic, and cumin, stir well, and cook for a few minutes. Add the beans and cooked rice, stir, and heat until warmed through.

4. Warm the tortillas and place ½ cup of the filling down the middle of each one. Add yogurt, cheese, and green onions. Fold the bottom up, then fold the sides over and roll the tortillas. Serve with salsa.

Southwestern Vegetable Wraps

Serves: 6

Ingredients:

- 1 can of rinsed, drained black beans (15 ounces)

- 2 large, seeded and diced tomatoes

- 1 cup of frozen-thawed corn

- 1 cup of cooked, cooled brown rice

- ¼ cup of fresh cilantro, minced

- 1/3 cup of fat-free sour cream

- 2 chopped shallots
- 1 seeded, chopped jalapeno pepper
- 2 tbsp of lime juice
- ½ tsp of chili powder
- ½ tsp of ground cumin
- ½ tsp of salt
- 6 whole romaine leaves
- 6 whole wheat tortillas (8-inch diameter)

Instructions:

1. Put the beans and rice in a bowl. Add the tomatoes, corn, cilantro, shallots, jalapeno, and sour cream and stir. Season with the lime juice, chili powder, salt, and cumin, and mix thoroughly.

2. Bring the tortillas to room temperature and lay a romaine leaf over each one. Top each one with 1/6th of the bean mixture, roll them up tight, and slice in half. If necessary, use toothpicks to secure them.

3. Leftovers may be refrigerated.

Black Bean and Sweet Potato Rice Bowls

Serves: 4

Ingredients:

- 1 peeled and diced large sweet potato
- 1 finely chopped red onion
- 4 cups of destemmed, shopped fresh kale
- 1 can of rinsed, drained black beans (15 ounces)

- ¾ cup of long-grain rice, uncooked
- 3 tbsp of olive oil
- 2 tbsp of sweet chili sauce
- 1 ½ cups of water
- ¼ tsp of garlic salt
- Lime wedges and sweet chili sauce for serving

Instructions:

1. Put the water in a large pan, add the rice and garlic salt, and bring to a boil. Turn the heat down, cover the pan, and simmer for 15 to 20 minutes until the rice is tender and the liquid has been absorbed. Take the pan off the heat and let it cool for 5 minutes.

2. Meanwhile, heat 2 tbsp oil in a large skillet over medium-high heat and cook the sweet potato for 8 minutes, stirring occasionally. Add the onion and cook for 4 to 6 minutes, stirring occasionally, until the potato is fork-tender.

3. Add the kale and cook for 3 to 5 minutes, stirring, until the kale is tender, then add the beans, stir, and cook until heated through.

4. Add the rest of the oil and 2 tbsp chili sauce to the rice and stir it through gently.

5. Add the rice to the potatoes, stir well, and serve with a little chili sauce and lime wedges.

Shrimp and Nectarine Salad

Serves: 4

Ingredients:

- 1/3 cup of fresh, natural orange juice
- 3 tbsp of apple cider vinegar
- 1 ½ tsp of organic honey
- 1 ½ tsp of Dijon mustard
- 1 tbsp of fresh tarragon, minced

For the Salad:

- 1 lb. of peeled, deveined, raw shrimp
- 4 tsp of canola oil
- 1 cup of frozen or fresh corn
- 8 cups of torn salad greens
- 2 medium nectarines, cut into 1-inch cubes
- 1 cup of halved grape or cherry tomatoes
- ½ cup of red onion, finely chopped
- ½ tsp of lemon-pepper seasoning
- ¼ tsp of salt

Instructions:

1. Whisk the orange juice, mustard, vinegar, and honey until well combined, and stir in the tarragon. Set aside.

2. Heat 1 tbsp of oil in a large skillet over medium-high heat and cook the corn, stirring frequently, for 1 to 2

minutes until tender but crisp. Remove the corn from the pan and set aside.

3. Mix the lemon pepper seasoning and salt and sprinkle it over the shrimp. Heat the rest of the oil in the skillet and cook the shrimp for 3 to 4 minutes, until pink, stirring frequently. Add the corn and stir it in.

4. Combine the salad greens, nectarine cubes, tomatoes, and onion in a large bowl and toss with 1/3 cup of the dressing. Divide between serving plates. Add the shrimp mixture on top, drizzle with the rest of the dressing, and serve immediately.

Fish Tacos

Serves: 6

Ingredients:

- 6 mahi mahi fillets (6 ounces each)
- ¼ cup of olive oil
- 2 cups of red cabbage, chopped
- 1 cup of fresh cilantro, chopped
- 1 tsp of ground cardamom
- 1 tsp of salt
- 1 tsp of paprika
- 1 tsp of pepper
- Salsa Verde – OPTIONAL
- 2 medium limes, chopped into even wedges
- 12 corn tortillas (6-inch diameter)
- Hot pepper sauce

Ingredients:

1. Place the olive oil, paprika, cardamom, salt, and pepper in a 13 x 9-inch baking dish and whisk thoroughly. Place the fillets in it, turn them to ensure they are coated, and cover the dish. Refrigerate for half an hour.

2. Lift the fish and discard the marinade. Oil a grill rack and heat it to medium-high heat. Place the fish on the rack, cover it, and cook for 4 to 5 minutes on each side until flaky. Remove the fish to a plate and set aside.

3. Heat the tortillas on the same rack for 30 to 45 seconds and keep them warm while you assemble them.

4. Divide the fish among them, and top with cabbage and cilantro. If using, add salsa Verde. Season with hot pepper sauce and lime juice, fold the sides over and serve warm with extra pepper sauce and lime wedges.

Lentil Medley

Serves: 8

Ingredients:

- 1 cup of dry lentils, rinsed
- 2 cups of water
- 2 cups of fresh mushrooms, sliced
- 1 cubed medium cucumber
- 1 cubed medium zucchini
- 1 chopped small red onion
- 4 cups of chopped baby spinach leaves
- 1 cup of feta cheese, crumbled

- 4 cooked, crumbled bacon strips - OPTIONAL
- ½ cup of sun-dried tomato halves, chopped (don't use the oil-packed tomatoes)
- ½ cup of rice wine vinegar
- ¼ cup of fresh mint, minced
- 3 tbsp of olive oil
- 2 tsp of organic honey
- 1 tsp of dried oregano
- 1 tsp of dried basil

Instructions:

1. Put the lentils in a pan, add the water, and bring to a boil over medium-high heat. Turn the heat down, cover the pan, and simmer until tender, about 20 to 25 minutes. Drain the lentils and rinse them under cold running water.

2. Place the lentils in a large bowl and add the cucumber, mushrooms, tomatoes, onion, and zucchini. Stir to combine.

3. Combine the vinegar, oil, mint, honey, oregano, and basil in a small bowl and drizzle it over the lentils. Toss to coat and stir in the cheese and spinach. Add the bacon if using, and toss to combine everything. Serve immediately.

California Quinoa Bowl

Serves: 4

Ingredients:

- 1 cup of rinsed, drained quinoa

- 1 tbsp of olive oil

- 1 minced garlic clove

- 1 chopped medium zucchini

- ¾ cup of rinsed, drained chickpeas or garbanzo beans

- 1 finely chopped medium tomato

- ½ cup of feta cheese, crumbled

- ¼ cup of Greek olives, finely chopped

- 2 tbsp of fresh basil, minced

- ¼ tsp of pepper

Instructions:

1. Heat the oil in a large pot over medium-high heat. Cook the garlic and quinoa, stirring frequently, for 2 to 3 minutes until the quinoa is turning light brown.

2. Add the water and zucchini, bring it to a boil, and turn the heat down. Cover the pot and simmer for 12 to 15 minutes until the liquid has been absorbed.

3. Add the beans, tomato, cheese, olives, and basil, season with the pepper and stir. Cook until everything is heated through, and serve hot.

Farro Salad with Roasted Vegetables

Serves: 4 to 6

Ingredients:

For the Salad:

- 1 lb. of peeled, deveined raw shrimp

- 1 cup of dry farro

- 1 yellow bell pepper, cut in half and deseeded
- 1 red bell pepper, cut in half and deseeded
- 1 red onion, chopped into chunks
- 2 sliced zucchini
- 2 cups of arugula
- 1 pint of cherry or grape tomatoes
- ½ cup of walnuts
- 2 tbsp of olive oil
- 1 tsp of Italian seasoning
- ¼ tsp of red chili flakes
- Salt and pepper

For the Dressing:
- 4 tbsp of natural orange juice
- 2 tbsp of chopped fresh parsley
- 1 tbsp of lemon juice
- 1 tbsp of olive oil
- ½ tsp of red chili flakes
- ½ tsp of Italian seasoning
- Salt and pepper

Instructions:
1. Preheat your oven to 450°F an line a baking sheet with parchment paper.
2. Cook the farro per the package instructions.

3. Place the pepper halves, zucchini, and onions on the baking sheet, drizzle with 1 tbsp of oil, and season to taste with salt and pepper. Roast for about 30 minutes, then set aside to cool down enough to handle. Dicen and set aside.

4. Combine all the dressing ingredients and season to taste.

5. Mix the Italian seasoning and chili flakes, season with salt and pepper, and sprinkle over the shrimp.

6. Heat the remaining oil over medium-high heat in a skillet and cook the shrimp on each side for 2 to 3 minutes. Transfer to a bowl.

7. Toss the farro, diced veggies, tomatoes, and walnuts in a bowl. Add 5 tbsp of dressing, toss to coat, and add the rest of the dressing to the shrimp. Stir to coat.

8. Lay the arugula on a large serving plate, add the farro mixture on top, and finish with the shrimp. Serve immediately.

Tabbouleh Salad

Serves: 6

Ingredients:

- ½ cup of uncooked bulgar wheat
- 2 bunches of finely chopped fresh parsley
- 1 cup of finely diced cucumber
- 1 cup of finely diced tomato
- 3 finely chopped scallions
- ¼ cup of finely chopped fresh mint

- ¼ cup of olive oil
- 2 tbsp of lemon juice
- Salt and pepper

Instructions:

1. Cook the bulgar per the package instructions, then drain it and leave it to cool down.

2. Put the lemon juice and olive oil in a bowl, season with salt and pepper, and whisk.

3. Put the cooked bulgur in a large bowl, add the mint, parsley, cucumber, and tomato, and stir to combine. Add the dressing, combine, and season to taste.

4. Serve immediately or chill it first.

Peppered Tuna Kabobs

Serves: 4

Ingredients:

- 1 lb. of tuna steak, cubed in 1-inch pieces
- ½ cup of frozen-thawed corn
- 4 chopped scallions
- 1 seeded and chopped jalapeno
- 2 tbsp of fresh parsley, coarsely chopped
- 2 tbsp of lime juice
- 2 large red peppers, chopped into 2 x 1-inch pieces
- 1 mango, peeled and chopped into 1-inch cubes
- 1 tsp of coarse-ground black pepper

- 4 soaked wooden skewers

Ingredients:

1. Make the salsa by combining the corn, scallions, jalapeno, lime juice, and parsley in a bowl.

2. Rub the pepper all over the tuna cubes. Alternate the tuna, mango, and pepper on each skewer until all the ingredients are used up.

3. Grease a grill rack, place the skewers on it, and cover them. Cook over medium heat, turning now and then, for 10 to 12 minutes, turning occasionally to cook them evenly. The tuna should be a little pink in the center still.

4. Serve hot with the salsa.

Warm Rice and Pintos Salad

Serves: 4

Ingredients:

- 8.8 ounce packet of ready-to-serve brown rice
- 1 cup of frozen corn kernels
- 1 chopped small onion
- 2 minced garlic cloves
- 1 can of rinsed, drained pinto beans (15 ounces)
- 1 can of chopped green chilies (4 ounces)
- 1 bunch romaine, sliced lengthwise into 4 (cut through the core)
- ¼ cup of cheddar cheese, finely shredded
- ½ cup salsa

- 1 tbsp of olive oil
- 1 ½ tsp of ground cumin
- 1 ½ tsp of chili powder

Instructions:

1. Heat the oil in a large skillet over medium-high heat.
2. Cook the onion and corn, stirring frequently, for 4 to 5 minutes until the onion softens. Add the chili powder, garlic, and cumin, stir, and cook for another minute.
3. Stir in the rice, beans, salsa, chili, and cilantro. Heat until hot all the way through, stirring now and then.
4. Serve over wedges of romaine lettuce and garnished with cheese.

Asparagus Soup

Serves: 12 (2 ¼ quarts)

Ingredients:

- 2 lb. of trimmed, fresh asparagus chopped into 1-inch pieces
- 6 cups of low-salt chicken or vegetable broth
- 2/3 cup of long-grain, uncooked brown rice
- 1 chopped medium onion
- 1 thinly sliced medium carrot
- 1 tbsp of butter
- 1 tbsp of olive oil
- ½ tsp of salt
- ¼ tsp of pepper

- ¼ tsp of dried thyme

- Low-fat sour cream – OPTIONAL

- Salad croutons – OPTIONAL

Instructions:

1. Heat the oil and butter in a 6-quart soup pot over medium heat. Add the asparagus, carrot, and onion, and season with salt, pepper, and thyme. Stir and cook for 8 to 10 minutes, stirring now and then, until the vegetables have softened a little.

2. Add the broth and rice and bring it to a boil. Turn the heat down, cover the pot, and simmer for 40 to 45 minutes until the rice is tender. Stir occasionally.

3. Use an immersion blender to puree the soup in the pot or let it cool down a little, and process in batches in a blender.

4. Heat the soup through and serve hot as is or with croutons and sour cream.

Sesame Chicken Veggie Wraps

Serves: 8

Ingredients:

- 1 cup of shelled edamame, frozen

For the Dressing:

- 2 tbsp of orange juice

- 2 tbsp of olive oil

- 1 tsp of sesame oil

- ½ tsp of ground ginger

- ¼ tsp of salt
- 1/8 tsp of pepper

For the Wraps:

- 2 cups of baby spinach leaves
- 1 cup of cucumber, thinly sliced
- 1 cup of sugar snap peas, chopped
- ½ cup of carrots, shredded
- ½ cup of sweet red pepper, thinly sliced
- 1 cup of cooked chicken breast, chopped
- 8 whole wheat tortillas (8-inch diameter)

Instructions:

1. Follow the packet instructions to cook the edamame, then drain and rinse them under running cold water. Set aside to drain thoroughly.

2. Make the dressing by combining the orange juice, olive oil, sesame oil, ginger, pepper, and salt, and whisk well.

3. Place the spinach, carrot, cucumber, red pepper, and sugar snap peas in a bowl, add the edamame and chicken, and stir to combine. Add the dressing and toss to combine.

4. Put ½ cup of the mixture onto each tortilla, fold the bottom and the sides, and roll the tortillas tightly.

5. Serve or refrigerate.

Mixed Vegetable Salad with Lime Dressing

Serves: 6

Ingredients:

- 2 cups of mixed veggies*
- ¼ cup of canola oil
- ¼ cup of olive oil
- 3 tbsp of lime juice
- 1 ½ tbsp of fresh cilantro, finely chopped
- ½ tsp of pepper
- ½ tsp of salt
- 6 romaine leaves
- 1 small bunch of destemmed watercress
- 1 sliced hard-boiled egg
- 1 thick red onion slice, separated into rings
- Crumbled feta, Mexican queso fresco, or farmer cheese for garnish

*Choose between raw vegetables, i.e., sliced radish, cucumber, tomato, etc., or steamed, i.e., beets, carrots, small potatoes, etc.

Instructions:

1. Whisk the olive and canola oil with the lime juice and cilantro. Season with salt and pepper and blend thoroughly.

2. Drop the mixed vegetables into the bowl and stir to coat them.

3. Place the lettuce on a large plate and add the veggies. Place the watercress around them and top with cheese, onion, and egg. Serve immediately or chill first.

Shredded Pork Salad

Serves: 12

Ingredients:

- 3 to 4 lb. of pork loin roast, boneless
- 1 ½ cup of apple juice or cider
- 1 can of drained chopped green chilies (4 ounces)
- 3 minced garlic cloves
- 1 can of rinsed, drained black beans (15 ounces)
- 2 chopped medium tomatoes
- 12 cups of torn salad greens
- 1 cup frozen or fresh corn kernels
- 1 chopped red onion
- 1 cup of Cotija (crumbled) OR part-skimmed mozzarella cheese (shredded)
- 1 ½ tsp of salt
- 1 ½ tsp of hot pepper sauce
- 1 tsp of chili powder
- 1 tsp of pepper
- ½ tsp of dried oregano
- ½ tsp of ground cumin
- Your choice of salad dressing

Instructions:

1. Put the pork in a large crockpot.

2. Combine the cider, garlic, green chilies, pepper sauce, salt, chili powder, pepper, oregano, and cumin in a small bowl. Whisk well and pour it over the pork. Put the lid on and cook for 6 to 8 hours on LOW until the meat is tender.

3. Lift the pork from the crockpot and discard the liquid. Use a pair of forks to shred the pork.

4. Place the salad greens on a platter, put the shredded pork on top, and add the beans, onion, tomato, corn, and cheese and garnish with salad dressing. Serve immediately.

Quinoa Power Salad

Serves: 2

Ingredients:

- 8 ounces of chicken tenders
- ½ cup of cooked and cooled red quinoa
- 1 peeled sweet potato, chopped into wedges (about ½-inch thick)
- ½ red onion, chopped into wedges (about ¼-inch thick)
- 2 tbsp of olive oil
- 2 tbsp of whole-grain mustard
- 1 tbsp of shallot, finely chopped
- 1 tbsp of organic maple syrup

- 1 tbsp of apple cider vinegar

- 4 cups of baby spinach, arugula, or kale, or a mixture

- 1 tbsp of toasted unsalted sunflower seeds

- ½ tsp of garlic powder

- ¼ tsp of salt

Instructions:

1. Preheat your oven to 425°F.

2. Put the onion and sweet potato in a bowl, add the garlic power, 1 tbsp oil, and 1/8 tsp salt. Toss to combine and spread it evenly on a large baking sheet. Roast it for 15 minutes.

3. While the veggies are roasting, put the chicken in a bowl, add 1 tbsp mustard, and stir to coat.

4. Take the veggies out of the oven, stir them, and put the chicken in the pan. Roast it for about 10 minutes, until the chicken is cooked and the veggies are starting to go brown. Take the pan out of the oven and set it aside to cool.

5. While it cools, combine the vinegar, maple syrup, shallot, 1 tbsp mustard, 1 tbsp olive oil, and the rest of the salt in a medium bowl, whisking well to combine.

6. Shred the chicken and add it to the dressing. Add the greens, roasted vegetables, and quinoa, toss to combine, and serve garnished with sunflower seeds.

Slow-Cooker Chicken and Chickpea Soup

Serves: 6

Ingredients:

- 2 lb. of trimmed, skinless chicken thighs, bone-in
- 1 can of drained artichoke hearts, quartered (14 ounces)
- 1 ½ cups of dried chickpeas*
- 4 cups of water
- 1 finely chopped large yellow onion
- 1 can of no-added-salt fire-roasted, diced tomatoes (15 ounces)
- ¼ cup of oil-cured olive, pitted and halved
- 2 tbsp of tomato paste
- 4 finely chopped garlic cloves
- 1 whole bay leaf
- 4 tsp of ground cumin
- 4 tsp of paprika
- ¼ tsp of black pepper
- ¼ tsp of cayenne pepper
- ¼ cup of fresh cilantro or parsley
- ½ tsp of salt

*Soak overnight.

Instructions:

1. Drain the soaked chickpeas and put them in a large crockpot. Add the water, tomatoes (plus juices), onion, garlic, tomato paste, cumin, bay leaf, paprika, black pepper, and cayenne. Stir, put the lid on, and cook for 8 hours on LOW or 4 hours on HIGH.

2. Preheat the oven to 400°F and place a sheet of aluminum foil and a backing rack on a baking tray. Place the chicken on the tray and bake for 35 to 45 minutes or until the internal temperature is 170°F.

3. Remove the chicken and place it on a cutting board. Leave to cool slightly. Shred it with a fork and discard the bones.

4. Lift the bay leaf from the slow cooker, stir the olives, artichokes, and salt in, and add the shredded chicken. Stir, heat through, and serve garnished with fresh herbs.

Beef and Bean Sloppy Joes

Serves: 4

Ingredients:

- 12 ounces of ground beef (90% lean)
- 1 tbsp of olive oil
- 1 cup of rinsed, drained, no-added-salt black beans
- 1 cup of onion, chopped
- 2 tsp of chili powder
- ½ tsp of onion powder
- ½ tsp of garlic powder

- Pinch of cayenne
- 1 cup of no-added-salt tomato sauce
- 3 tbsp of tomato ketchup
- 1 tbsp of low-salt Worcestershire sauce
- 2 tsp of spicy brown mustard
- 1 tsp of brown sugar
- 4 split and toasted whole wheat burger buns

Instructions:

1. Heat the oil over medium-high heat in a large skillet.

2. Cook the beef for 3 to 4 minutes, until light brown but not fully cooked, stirring with a wooden spoon to break it down.

3. Lift the beef using a slotted spoon and put it in a bowl. Leave the cooking juice in the pan.

4. Add the onions and beans to the pan, and cook for about 5 minutes, until the onion is tender. Stir often to stop the beans from sticking.

5. Stir in the chili powder, onion powder, garlic powder, and cayenne, and cook for about 30 seconds until fragrant, stirring frequently. Add the ketchup, tomato sauce, mustard, Worcestershire sauce, and brown sugar and stir it in.

6. Add the beef, let the mixture come to a simmer, and cook for about 5 minutes, stirring frequently, until the beef is cooked through and the sauce is a little thicker.

7. Serve hot on bun halves.

No-Cook Black Bean Salad

Serves: 4

Ingredients:

- ½ cup of red onion, thinly sliced
- 1 pitted ripe avocado, chopped roughly
- ¼ cup of fresh cilantro leaves
- ¼ cup of lime juice
- 2 tbsp of olive oil
- 1 minced garlic clove
- 8 cups of salad greens
- 2 cups of frozen-thawed corn kernels, patted dry
- 1 pint of halved grape or cherry tomatoes
- 1 can of rinsed, drained black beans (15 ounces)
- ½ tsp of salt

Instructions:

1. Put the onion in a bowl, add enough cold water to cover it, and put it aside.

2. Place the avocado, lime juice, cilantro, garlic, oil, and salt in a small food processed and process to a smooth, creamy consistency. Scrape the sides down as needed to ensure all the ingredients are incorporated.

3. Mix the salad greens, tomatoes, corn, beans, and tomatoes in a bowl. Drain the onions, add them to the bowl, and top with the avocado dressing. Stir to combine and serve immediately, or chill first.

Slow-Cooker Pasta e Fagioli Soup

Serves: 6

Ingredients:

- 1 lb. of skinless, boneless chicken thighs
- 1 can of rinsed, drained, no-added-salt white beans (15 ounces)
- 4 cups of baby spinach
- 4 tbsp of fresh basil, chopped
- ½ cup of Parmigiano-Reggiano cheese, shredded
- 2 tbsp of olive oil
- 2 cups of chopped onion
- 1 cup of chopped celery
- 1 cup of chopped carrot
- 4 cups of whole wheat rotini pasta
- 6 cups of low-salt chicken broth
- 4 tsp of Italian seasoning
- ¼ tsp of salt

Instructions:

1. Preheat your oven to 400°F and place parchment paper on a baking tray. Roast the chicken for 18 to 22 minutes until cooked through, then set aside to cool. Chop into small pieces.

2. Cook the pasta per the package instructions, then drain and set aside to cool.

3. Place the broth in a large crockpot and add the onions, carrots, and celery. Stir in the salt and Italian seasoning, put the lid on, and cook on LOW for 7 ¼ hours.

4. Stir in the spinach, beans, half the basil, pasta, and chicken. Put the lid back on and cook for 45 minutes until hot through.

5. Serve hot with a drizzle of oil, cheese, and fresh basil.

Salmon Couscous Salad

Serves: 1

Ingredients:

- 4 ounces of cooked salmon fillet
- ¼ cup of cooked whole wheat Israeli couscous
- ¼ cup of cremini mushrooms, sliced
- ¼ cup of eggplant, diced
- 3 cups of baby spinach leaves
- ¼ cup of dried, sliced apricots
- 2 tbsp of crumbled goat or feta cheese

For the Dressing:

- 2 tbsp of white wine vinegar
- 1/8 tsp of salt
- 1/8 tsp of black pepper
- ¼ cup of olive oil

Instructions:

1. Make the dressing. Combine the vinegar, salt, and pepper, and gradually whisk the oil in until thoroughly blended.

2. Spray cooking spray over a small skillet and heat it over medium-high heat. Cook the eggplant and mushrooms, stirring occasionally, for about 3 to 5 minutes until they release their juices and turn light brown. Take the pan off the heat and set it aside.

3. Put the spinach in a bowl, add 1 tbsp and 1 tsp of vinaigrette, and toss to coat. Put it on a large serving plate.

4. Add 2 tsp of vinaigrette to the couscous, stir to combine, and spoon it on top of the spinach. Top with the salmon, vegetables, apricots, and cheese. Serve immediately.

Mushroom-Swiss Turkey Burgers

Serves: 4

Ingredients:

- 8 portobello mushrooms, gills, and stems removed*
- 1 lb. of lean ground turkey
- 2 tbsp of olive oil
- 1 minced garlic clove
- 2 tsp of Worcestershire sauce (gluten-free if possible)
- 1 tsp of Dijon mustard
- ¾ tsp of ground black pepper
- ½ tsp of salt

- 4 slices of Swiss cheese

- 1 thinly sliced small tomato

- 3 cups of baby arugula leaves

Instructions:

1. Preheat a grill to 400 to 450°F.

2. Mix the oil with the garlic, ¼ tsp salt, and ¼ tsp pepper, and brush it over the mushroom caps. Set them aside for 10 minutes.

3. Place the ground turkey in a bowl, and add the mustard, Worcestershire sauce, ¼ tsp salt, and ½ tsp of pepper. Mix gently and shape it into 4 patties, each ¾-inch thick. Set them aside.

4. Brush oil over the grill rack** and lay the mushrooms on it, cap-side down. Cover them and grill for 4 minutes before turning them over and grilling for 4 minutes on the other side. Place them on a plate and cover them to keep them warm.

5. Brush more oil on the rack and place the four patties on it. Cover and cook them for 5 minutes on each side. The patties should be just charred, and the internal temperature should be 165°F. Place a slice of cheese on each patty a minute before the final cooking time is up.

6. Place the patties on a plate and let them stand for 5 minutes. If you have a large enough grill, you can save time by cooking the patties and mushrooms at the same time.

7. Place a turkey patty on top of the open side of four mushrooms. Add slices of tomato and some arugula,

and place another mushroom cap on top. Serve immediately.

* To clean the mushrooms, twist the stem off gently and scrape out the gills using a spoon.

** Oiling the racks means the food won't stick. The best way to do it is to use a piece of kitchen towel dipped in oil. Holding it with tongs, rub it over the grill racks. Never use cooking spray.

Stuffed Sweet Potato with Hummus Dressing

Serves: 1

Ingredients:

- 1 large, scrubbed sweet potato
- ¾ cup of roughly chopped kale
- 1 cup of rinsed, drained black beans
- ¼ cup of hummus
- 2 tbsp of water

Instructions:

1. Use a fork to prick the potato all over, and microwave on HIGH for 7 to 10 minutes until cooked through.

2. While the potato is cooking, wash and drain the kale, but let some water stick to the leaves. Put the kale in a saucepan and put the lid on. Cook for a couple of minutes, stirring two or three times, until the kale is wilted.

3. Add the beans and add up to 2 tbsp of water if the pot is dry. Cook for 1 to 2 minutes until everything is piping hot, stirring occasionally.

4. Split the potato and fill it with beans and kale. Mix 2 tbsp of water and the hummus, adding extra water if needed to get the desired consistency.

5. Drizzle it over the potato and serve hot.

Chipotle Chicken Quinoa Burrito Bowl

Serves: 4

Ingredients:

- 1 lb. of skinless, boneless chicken breast
- 1 tbsp of chipotle peppers in adobo sauce, finely chopped
- 1 tbsp of olive oil
- 2 cups of cooked quinoa
- 2 cups of romaine lettuce, shredded
- 1 cup of rinsed, drained pinto beans
- 1 diced ripe avocado
- ¼ cup of salsa
- ¼ cup of Monterey Jack or cheddar cheese, shredded
- ½ tsp of ground cumin
- ½ tsp of garlic powder
- ¼ tsp of salt
- Lime wedges to serve

Instructions:

1. Preheat the broiler or grill to medium-high.

---

2. Place the chipotle peppers in a bowl, add the cumin, garlic powder, and oil, and mix well.

3. Oil the grill rack or brush oil over a baking sheet if using the broiler.

4. Season the chicken with the salt and grill on one side for 5 minutes or broil for 9 minutes. Turn the chicken over, brush the chipotle glaze over it, and grill for 3 to 5 minutes or broil for 9 minutes, until the internal temperature on a meat thermometer reads 165°F.

5. Place the chicken on a chopping board and slice it into small pieces.

6. Place ½ cup cooked quinoa in each bowl, add ½ a cup each of the chicken and lettuce, ¼ cup of beans, and top with 1 tbsp each of salsa and cheese.

7. Serve straight away with a lime wedge.

White Bean Soup

Serves: 6

Ingredients:

- 2 cans of rinsed, drained Great Northern beans (15 ½ ounces each)
- 1 cup of rinsed, drained canned corn kernels
- 2 cups of baby spinach leaves
- 6 cups of low-salt chicken or vegetable broth
- 1 tbsp of olive oil
- 1 tbsp of butter
- 1 diced small onion

- 1 peeled large carrot, sliced widthwise
- 3 sliced celery stalks
- ¼ cup of fresh parsley, chopped
- 4 minced garlic cloves
- 1 tsp of salt
- ½ tsp of black pepper
- ½ tsp of dried oregano
- 1 whole bay leaf
- Grated parmesan cheese for garnish
- Toasted bread slices for garnish

Instructions:

1. Put the butter and olive oil in a large stockpot or Dutch oven and heat it over medium-high heat.

2. Add the celery, carrots, onions, and parsley, and cook until just starting to soften, about 5 minutes. Add the garlic, stir, and cook for 30 seconds.

3. Add the broth, season with salt, pepper, and oregano, and drop the bay leaf in. Bring it to a boil and turn the heat down. Simmer for 5 minutes.

4. Add the corn and beans and cook for 5 minutes, stirring occasionally. Season with salt and pepper to taste.

5. Add the spinach, cook for a minute, then remove the pot from the heat.

6. Serve hot, garnished with parmesan cheese and with toasted bread on the side.

DINNER

White Wine Garlic Chicken

Serves: 4

Ingredients:

- 4 skinless, boneless chicken breasts (6 ounces each)
- ½ cup of low-salt chicken broth OR dry white wine
- 2 cups of baby portobello mushrooms, sliced
- 1 chopped medium onion
- 2 minced garlic cloves
- ½ tsp of salt
- ¼ tsp of black pepper
- 1 tbsp of olive oil

Instructions:

1. Wrap each chicken breast in plastic wrap and use a meat mallet to flatten it to ½-inch thick.

2. Season them with salt and pepper and set aside.

3. Heat the oil in a large skillet over medium heat and cook the chicken for 5 to 6 minutes on each side until cooked through. Lift them from the pan and set them aside, covered in foil to keep warm.

4. Cook the onions and mushrooms over high heat for 2 to 3 minutes until light brown and tender, stirring frequently.

5. Add the garlic, cook for 30 seconds, stirring, and then add the wine or broth. Bring it to a boil, stirring with a wooden spoon to deglaze the pan, and cook until the liquid has reduced slightly.

6. Serve the chicken with the mushroom sauce.

Shrimp Orzo with Feta

Serves: 4

Ingredients:

- 1 ¼ cups of whole wheat orzo, uncooked
- 1 ¼ lb. of peeled, deveined uncooked shrimp
- 2 tbsp of olive oil
- 2 minced garlic cloves
- 2 chopped medium tomatoes
- 2 tbsp of lemon juice
- ½ cup of feta cheese, crumbled
- 2 tbsp of fresh cilantro, minced
- ¼ tsp of black pepper

Instructions:

1. Cook the pasta following the packaging instructions.

2. While it is cooking, heat the oil over medium heat in a large skillet. Cook the garlic for a minute, stirring frequently.

3. Add the lemon juice and tomatoes, and bring it to a boil. Add the shrimp, stir, and turn the heat down. Simmer for 4 to 5 minutes until the shrimp has turned pink.

4. Drain the orzo and add it to the shrimp. Stir it in and heat until hot through.

5. Serve sprinkled with cheese.

Cherry-Chicken Lettuce Wraps

Serves: 4

Ingredients:

- ¾ lb. of skinless, boneless chicken breast
- 1 ½ cups of grated carrot
- 1 ¼ cups of sweet cherries, pitted and roughly chopped
- 4 chopped scallions
- 1/3 cup of almonds, coarsely chopped
- 2 tbsp of rice wine vinegar
- 2 tbsp of low-sodium teriyaki sauce
- 1 tbsp of organic honey
- 8 Boston or Bibb lettuce leaves
- 1 tsp of ground ginger
- ¼ tsp of black pepper
- ¼ tsp of salt
- 2 tsp of olive oil

Ingredients:

1. Chop the chicken into ¾-inch cubes and place it in a shallow dish. Sprinkle the salt, pepper, and ginger over and toss to coat the chicken.

---

2. Heat a skillet over medium-high, add the oil, and cook the chicken for 3 to 5 minutes until cooked through.

3. Take the chicken off the heat, and add the grated carrot, onions, cherries, and almonds. Stir to combine.

4. Mix the teriyaki sauce, vinegar, and honey and add to the chicken. Stir to coat the chicken and spoon onto the lettuce leaves.

5. Fold each leaf over the filling and serve straight away.

Peanut Ginger Linguine

Serves: 4

Ingredients:

- 8 ounces of whole wheat linguine, uncooked
- 2 cups of small broccoli florets
- 2 grated medium carrots
- 1 julienned sweet red pepper
- 2 chopped scallions
- 2 tbsp of minced fresh basil
- ¼ cup of lime juice
- 2 ½ tsp of grated lime zest
- 2 tbsp of low-salt soy sauce
- 2 tsp of water
- 1/3 cup of creamy, smooth peanut butter
- 1 tsp of sesame oil
- 2 minced garlic cloves

- 2 ½ tsp of fresh ginger root, minced
- ¼ tsp of black pepper
- ¼ tsp of salt

Instructions:

1. Cook the linguine following the package instructions.

2. Put the lime juice, zest, soy sauce, water, sesame oil, peanut butter, ginger root, and minced garlic in a blender and blend to a smooth sauce.

3. Add the broccoli to the linguine 5 minutes before the end of the cooking time, then drain it and place it in a large bowl.

4. Season with salt and pepper, add the carrot, red pepper, basil, and onions, and stir together.

5. Pour in the peanut mixture, toss, and serve immediately.

Black Bean Pasta

Serves: 6

Ingredients:

- 9 ounces of whole wheat fettuccine, uncooked
- 1 ¾ cups of baby Portobello mushrooms, sliced
- 1 can of rinsed, drained black beans (15 ounces)
- 1 can of diced tomatoes with juices (approx. 15 ounces)
- 1 tbsp of olive oil
- 1 minced garlic clove
- 1 tsp of crushed fresh rosemary

- ½ tsp of dried oregano

- 2 cups of baby spinach leaves

Instructions:

1. Cook the fettuccine following the packet instructions.

2. Heat the oil in a large skillet over medium-high and cook the mushrooms for 4 to 6 minutes, until tender. Stir frequently. Stir in the garlic and cook for a minute.

3. Add the tomatoes, black beans, oregano, and rosemary. Stir and cook until heated through. Add the spinach and cook until it is wilted.

4. Drain the cooked fettuccine, add it to the pan, and toss to combine everything.

5. Serve immediately.

Cabbage Roll Skillet

Serves: 6

Ingredients:

- 1 can of whole plum tomatoes with juices (28 ounces)

- 1 lb. of 95% lean ground beef

- 1 chopped large onion

- 1 can of low-salt, low-sugar tomato sauce (8 ounces)

- 1 small whole cabbage, sliced thinly

- 1 thinly sliced green pepper

- 4 cups of cooked brown rice – hot

- 2 tbsp of apple cider vinegar

- 1 tbsp of soft brown sugar

- 1 tsp of dried thyme

- 1 tsp of dried oregano

- ½ tsp of black pepper

Instructions:

1. Cook the rice as per the package instructions and keep it hot.

2. Drain the tomatoes, setting the liquid aside, and chop them coarsely.

3. Heat a little oil over medium-high in a large skillet and cook the beef for 6 to 8 minutes, stirring constantly with a wooden spoon to break it down. Add the pepper, onion, sugar, tomato sauce, chopped tomatoes, tomato liquid, vinegar, and seasonings. Stir to combine.

4. Add the shredded cabbage and cover the pan. Cook for about 6 minutes, stirring occasionally. Remove the lid and cook for 6 to 8 minutes until the cabbage has softened.

5. Serve over the rice.

Butternut Linguine

Serves: 4

Ingredients:

- 4 cups of peeled butternut squash cubes

- 1 chopped red onion

- 2 cups of Swiss chard, julienned

- 3 tbsp of olive oil

- ½ lb. of uncooked linguine

- 1 tbsp of fresh sage, minced

- ½ tsp of salt

- ¼ tsp of pepper flakes

- ¼ tsp of pepper

Instructions:

1. Preheat your oven to 350°F and coat a 15 x 10 x 1-inch baking dish with cooking spray.

2. Lay the onion and butternut cubes evenly on the bottom of the dish. Mix the pepper flakes and olive oil and drizzle it over the vegetables. Toss to coat and bake until tender, about 45 to 50 minutes, stirring occasionally.

3. While the squash is cooking, cook the linguine, following the packet directions. Drain it, place it into a large bowl, and add the cooked veggies. Stir in the sage and Swiss chard, season with the salt and pepper, and toss. Serve immediately

Pork Chops with Tomato Curry

Serves: 6

Ingredients:

- 6 boneless pork loin chops (about 6 ounces each)

- 4 tsp of butter

- 1 finely chopped small onion

- 3 thinly sliced apples

- 1 can of whole tomatoes with juices (28 ounces)

- 4 tsp of sugar

- 2 tsp of curry powder

- ½ tsp of chili powder

- ½ tsp of salt

- 4 cups of cooked brown rice

- 2 tbsp of slivered almonds, toasted – OPTIONAL

Instructions:

1. Cook the rice following the packet directions.

2. Heat 2 tsp butter in a 6-qt soup pot over medium-high and brown the pork chops all over. Work in batches and lift them from the pan as they cook.

3. Add the rest of the butter to the pot, and cook the onions for 2 to 3 minutes until tender, stirring frequently. Add the apples, sugar, tomatoes (including juices), chili powder, salt, and curry powder. Bring it to a boil, stirring frequently to break the tomatoes down.

4. Add the chops and turn the heat down. Simmer for 5 minutes, then turn the pork over and cook for another 3 to 5 minutes. The internal temperature should be 145°F – use a meat thermometer to check.

5. Leave it for 5 minutes, then serve over the rice garnished with almonds.

Thai Chicken Pasta Skillet

Serves: 6

Ingredients:

- 6 ounces of whole wheat spaghetti, uncooked

- 10 ounces of trimmed sugar snap peas, sliced thinly in diagonal strips

- 2 cups of carrots, julienned

- 2 cups of cooked chicken, shredded

- 1 cup of Thai peanut sauce

- 1 cucumber, halved widthwise, deseeded and sliced thinly in diagonal strips

- 2 tsp of canola oil

- Chopped cilantro -OPTIONAL

Instructions:

1. Cook the spaghetti following the package directions, and drain it.

2. While it cooks, heat the oil in a large skillet over medium-high, and cook the carrots and snap peas for 6 to 8 minutes – they should be tender yet still crispy.

3. Add the chicken to the pan and stir in the peanut sauce, coating the chicken and vegetables.

4. Add the spaghetti, stir, and heat through, tossing to mix everything.

5. Serve garnished with cucumber and cilantro.

Sausage-Stuffed Zucchini

Serves: 6

Ingredients:

- 6 medium zucchini

- 1 lb. of Italian sausage links

- 2 seeded and chopped medium tomatoes
- 1 cup of panko breadcrumbs
- 1/3 cup of parmesan cheese, grated
- 1/3 cup of fresh parsley, minced
- 2 tbsp of fresh oregano, minced OR 2 tsp dried oregano
- 2 tbsp of fresh basil, minced OR 2 tsp dried basil
- ¼ tsp of black pepper
- ¾ cup of part-skim mozzarella, shredded
- Fresh parsley, minced – OPTIONAL

Instructions:

1. Preheat your oven to 350°F.

2. Remove the sausage meat from the casings and set aside.

3. Slice the zucchinis in half lengthwise and scoop the flesh out. Put the shells on a microwave-safe dish and cover. Cook for 2 to 3 minutes on HIGH until crisp but tender. Do this in batches if you need to.

4. Heat a large skillet over medium heat and cook the sausage meat and zucchini flesh for 6 to 8 minutes, until the sausage is cooked. Stir frequently with a wooden spoon to break the sausage meat down and drain the mixture.

5. Add the tomatoes, parmesan cheese, panko, pepper, and herbs, and divide the mixture between the shells.

6. Bake on ungreased baking dishes, covered, until the zucchini has softened, about 15 to 20 minutes. Sprinkle

the mozzarella cheese over the top and bake it for 5 to 8 minutes until it melts.

7. Serve garnished with minced fresh parsley.

Peppered Sole

Serves: 4

Ingredients:

- 4 sole fillets (about 4 ounces each)
- 2 cups of mushrooms, sliced
- 2 minced garlic cloves
- 1 chopped medium tomato
- 2 thinly sliced green onions
- 2 tbsp of butter
- ¼ tsp of paprika
- ¼ tsp of lemon-pepper
- 1/8 tsp of cayenne pepper

Instructions:

1. Heat the butter in a large skillet over medium-high and cook the mushrooms until tender, stirring occasionally. Add the garlic and cook for a minute.

2. Lay the sole fillets over the mushrooms and season with cayenne, lemon pepper, and paprika.

3. Cover the pan, reduce the heat to medium, and cook for 5 to 10 minutes until the fish is flaky.

4. Serve garnished with tomato and green onions.

Citrus-Herb Pork Roast

Serves: 8

Ingredients:

- 3 to 4 lb. of pork sirloin roast
- 2 medium onions, sliced into thin wedges
- 1 tsp of dried oregano
- ½ tsp of pepper
- ½ tsp of ground ginger
- 1 cup + 3 tbsp of orange juice
- 1 tbsp of sugar
- 1 tbsp of white grapefruit juice
- 1 tbsp of low-salt soy sauce
- 1 tbsp of steak sauce
- 3 tbsp of cornstarch
- 1 tsp of grated orange zest
- ½ tsp of salt
- Egg noodles, cooked
- Fresh oregano, minced – OPTIONAL

Instructions:

1. Slice the roast in half.
2. Mix the ginger, oregano, and pepper in a small bowl and rub it all over the pork.

3. Heat cooking spray in a large skillet and brown the two pieces of pork all over. Place them in a slow cooker and add the onions.

4. Mix 1 cup of orange juice, all the grapefruit juice, sugar, soy sauce, and steak sauce, and pour it over the pork. Put the lid on and cook on LOW until the meat is tender, about 4 to 5 hours. Lift the meat and onions out and place them on a serving platter. Cover with foil to keep warm.

5. Remove the fat from the cooking juices and discard. Pour the juices into a small pan and stir in the salt and orange zest. Bring it to a boil. Mix the cornstarch with the remaining orange juice until smooth, and stir it into the hot liquid. Let it come to a boil again and cook, stirring frequently, until thick, about 2 minutes.

6. While everything is cooking, cook egg noodles and serve hot with the pork and sauce, garnished with fresh oregano.

Creamy Lemon Pasta with Shrimp

Serves: 4

Ingredients:

- 8 ounces of uncooked whole wheat fettuccine
- 7 cups of water
- 12 ounces of deveined, peeled, uncooked shrimp
- 1 tbsp of olive oil
- 2 tbsp of unsalted butter
- 1 tbsp of garlic, finely chopped

- ¼ tsp of crushed red pepper flakes

- 4 loosely packed cups of arugula

- ¼ cup of plain fat-free yogurt

- 2 tbsp of lemon juice

- 1 tsp of lemon zest

- 1/3 cup of grated Parmesan + extra for garnish

- ¼ cup of fresh basil, sliced thinly

- ¼ tsp of salt

Instructions:

1. Bring the water to a boil and cook the fettuccine for 7 to 9 minutes until just starting to soften. Stir it frequently to stop the noodles from sticking together. Drain the noodles, but reserve ½ a cup of the liquid.

2. While the noodles cook, heat the oil over medium-high heat in a large skillet and cook the shrimp for 2 to 3 minutes until curled and pink. Stir occasionally to stop it from burning. When cooked, transfer it to a bowl and set aside.

3. Turn the heat down to medium, add the butter, and cook the garlic, stirring in the red pepper. Stir frequently for about a minute until the garlic is fragrant. Add the arugula and cook until wilted, about a minute,

4. Reduce the heat to low, and add the cooked fettuccine, reserved water, and lemon zest. Toss well until the fettucine is completely coated in a creamy sauce.

5. Add the shrimp and lemon juice, stir in the salt, and toss to coat.

6. Remove the pan from the heat and toss with the parmesan.

7. Serve hot, garnished with fresh basil and more parmesan.

Slow-Cooker Vegetarian Bolognese

Serves: 8

Ingredients:

- 1 lb. of whole wheat spaghetti
- 1 can of diced tomatoes (28 ounces)
- 2 cans of rinsed, drained, no-added salt cannellini or small white beans
- 1 cup of chopped onion
- ½ cup of chopped celery
- ½ cup of chopped carrot
- ½ cup of dry white wine
- ½ cup of water OR low-salt vegetable broth
- ½ cup of parmesan cheese, grated
- ¼ cup of fresh basil, chopped
- ¼ cup of heavy cream
- 3 tbsp of olive oil
- 1 tsp of Italian seasoning
- 2 tbsp of minced garlic
- ½ tsp of salt
- ¼ tsp of black pepper

Instructions:

1. Place the tomatoes, broth or water, wine, carrots, onion, and celery in a large crock pot. Stir in the salt, pepper, and Italian seasoning. Put the lid on and cook on LOW for 8 hours.

2. Lift the lid, stir the cream and beans in, and put the lid back on. Turn the crock pot to the Keep Warm setting.

3. Bring a large pot of water to a boil, add the spaghetti, and cook following the package instructions. Drain it, divide it between 8 bowls, and serve with the veggie sauce, parmesan, and fresh basil.

Roasted Salmon with Smoky Chickpeas and Greens

Serves: 4

Ingredients:

- 1 ¼ lb. of wild salmon, sliced into 4 equal pieces
- ¼ cup of water
- 10 cups of roughly chopped kale
- ¼ cup of fresh chives and/or dill, chopped + extra for garnish
- 1 can of drained and rinsed no-added-salt chickpeas (15 ounces)
- ¼ cup of low-fat mayonnaise
- 1/3 cup of buttermilk
- 2 tbsp of olive oil
- 1 tbsp of smoked paprika

- ½ tsp + a pinch of salt

- ½ tsp of ground black pepper

- ¼ tsp of garlic powder

Instructions:

1. Preheat your oven to 425°F and set racks in the middle and the top third.

2. Mix 1 tbsp olive oil with the paprika and ¼ tsp salt. Pat the chickpeas as dry as possible and add them to the paprika. Toss to combine. Spread the mixture over a baking sheet and bake for 30 minutes at the top of the oven, stirring twice during cooking time.

3. In the meantime, place the mayonnaise, buttermilk, fresh herbs, garlic powder, and ¼ tsp of pepper in a blender and process to a smooth consistency. Set aside.

4. Heat the remaining oil over medium heat in a large skillet and cook the kale for 2 minutes, stirring occasionally. Add the water and cook for 5 minutes, until the kale has softened. Take the pan off the heat, add a pinch of salt, and stir it.

5. Push the cooked chickpeas to one side of the baking tray and lay the salmon on the other side. Season with the rest of the salt and pepper and bake for 5 to 8 minutes, until it is just cooked through.

6. Serve the salmon drizzled with the dressing, chickpeas, and kale garnished with fresh herbs.

Kedjenou Chicken

Serves: 4

Ingredients:

- 4 to 6 skinless, boneless chicken breasts
- 2 medium onions
- 3 bell peppers – any color
- 4 medium tomatoes
- 1 small eggplant
- 4 scallions
- 1 ½ tbsp of chopped fresh ginger
- 1 ½ tbsp of chopped fresh garlic
- 2 whole bay leaves
- 8 to 10 sprigs of fresh thyme OR 1 tsp dried thyme
- 2 to 3 hot peppers
- 1 tsp of smoked paprika
- 1 chicken bouillon cube – low-salt
- Salt and pepper

Instructions:

1. Chop the onions, bell peppers, and scallions, and finely dice the ginger and garlic. Remove the skin from the chicken if there is any.

2. Place the chopped veggies, whole hot peppers, chicken, ginger, and garlic in a bowl and combine. Add the paprika, bay leaves, and thyme, season with salt and

pepper, and toss to combine. Cover and marinate for 2 hours or more.

3. Lift the chicken, bay leaves, and hot peppers from the bowl and set them aside. Chop the eggplant and add it to the bowl, stirring to combine.

4. Place half the mixture in a large Dutch oven and place the chicken on top. Add the bay leaves and hot peppers, then a few sprigs of fresh thyme. Season to taste, crumble the bouillon cube over the top, and then add the rest of the veggie mix.

5. Put a lid on the oven and cook over medium heat for 15 minutes. Turn the heat down to medium-low, and cook for 45 minutes. Shake the pot a few times during cooking, but do NOT take the lid off. When the time is up, check the chicken is tender – it should be fall-apart tender. If not, continue cooking for a few minutes.

6. Serve hot.

Salmon Cakes

Serves: 4

Ingredients:

- 15 ounces of drained canned salmon OR 1 ½ cups of cooked salmon

- 1 ¾ cups of wholewheat bread crumbs – fresh

- 1 finely diced celery stalk

- 1 finely chopped small onion

- 3 tsp of olive oil

- 2 tbsp of fresh parsley, finely chopped

- 1 whole egg

- 1 ½ tsp of Dijon mustard

- ½ tsp of black pepper

- 1 lemon, cut into 4 quarters

For the Sauce:

- ¼ cup of low-fat mayonnaise

- ¼ cup of plain nonfat yogurt

- 2 thinly sliced scallions

- 1 tbsp of lemon juice

- 1 tbsp of fresh dill, finely chopped

- Black pepper

Instructions:

1. Preheat your oven to 450°F and spray cooking spray over a large rimmed baking tray.

2. Heat 1 ½ tsp of oil over medium-high heat in a large skillet and cook the celery and onion for about 3 minutes, until soft. Add the parsley, stir it in, and take the pan off the heat.

3. Put the salmon in a bowl and use a fork to flake it, discarding any skin and bones. Add the mustard and the egg and mix thoroughly. Stir in the breadcrumbs and onion, mix well, and form it into 8 equal-sized patties.

4. Heat the rest of the oil over medium heat and cook 4 patties on one side for 2 to 3 minutes until golden brown. Lift them onto the baking tray and cook the other 4.

5. Bake for 15 to 20 minutes, until cooked through and golden brown on top.

6. While the patties are cooking, mix the sauce ingredients together. Serve the patties on a bed of spinach with the sauce and garnished with lemon.

Sweet Potato Carbonara with Spinach and Mushrooms

Serves: 5

Ingredients:

- 2 lb. of peeled sweet potatoes
- 3 whole eggs
- 1 cup of parmesan cheese, grated
- 3 chopped strips of center-cut bacon
- 8 ounces of mushrooms, sliced
- 5 ounces of baby spinach leaves
- 2 minced garlic cloves
- 1 tbsp of olive oil
- ¼ tsp of salt
- ¼ tsp of pepper

Instructions:

1. Bring a large pot of water to a boil.

2. Slice the sweet potatoes lengthwise using a julienne peeler or standard vegetable peeler. You want about 12 cups of long, thin strands.

3. Drop the potato strands into the boiling water and cook for about 1 ½ to 3 minutes, stirring a couple of times, until they start to go soft. Drain them, but reserve ¼ cup of the cooking liquid.

4. Put the "noodles" back in the pot but not on the heat.

5. Beat the eggs and whisk in the salt, pepper, parmesan, and reserved cooking liquid. Pour it over the potato noodles and toss gently to coat.

6. Heat the oil over medium heat in a large skillet and cook the mushrooms and bacon for about 6 to 8 minutes, until all the liquid is gone and the mushrooms begin to brown.

7. Add the garlic, cook for a minute until fragrant, and add the spinach. Cook for another minute or two, stirring frequently, until the spinach has wilted.

8. Transfer the vegetable mix to the noodles, toss, and serve seasoned with black pepper.

Sheet-Pan Chili-Lime Salmon with Potatoes and Peppers

Serves: 4

Ingredients:

- 1 lb. of Yukon Gold potatoes
- 1 ¼ lb. of center-cut salmon fillet
- 2 sliced bell peppers, any color
- 1 lime
- 2 tbsp of olive oil
- ¾ tsp of salt

- ¼ tsp of black pepper
- 2 tsp of chili powder
- 1 tsp of ground cumin
- ½ tsp of garlic powder

Instructions:

1. Preheat your oven to 425°F and spray cooking oil over a large baking tray.

2. Chop the potatoes into ¾-inch chunks and remove the skin from the salmon. Slice the salmon into 4 equal pieces. Grate the zest off the lime and set aside, and quarter the lime.

3. Put the potatoes in a bowl with 1 tbsp of olive oil and ¼ tsp each of salt and pepper. Toss to combine and transfer to the prepared baking tray. Roast for about 15 minutes.

4. Meanwhile, mix the cumin, chili powder, garlic, lime zest, and the rest of the salt. Put the bell peppers into a separate bowl, and add the rest of the olive oil and ½ tbsp of the chili mixture. Toss to coat the peppers, and use the rest of the spice mixture to coat the salmon.

5. Remove the roasted potatoes from the oven, stir in the peppers, and roast for 5 minutes. Take the pan from the oven.

6. Move some of the mixture to one side and place the salmon fillets on the pan. Roast for 6 to 8 minutes, until the salmon is cooked through, and serve hot on a bed of spinach with lime wedges.

One-Pot Garlicky Shrimp and Spinach

Serves: 4

Ingredients:

- 1 lb. of peeled, deveined shrimp
- 1 lb. of spinach leaves
- 3 tbsp of olive oil
- 6 sliced garlic cloves
- ¼ tsp of salt + 1/8 tsp
- 1 tbsp of lemon juice
- ¼ tsp of crushed red pepper flakes
- 1 tbsp of fresh parsley, finely chopped
- 1 ½ tsp of lemon zest

Instructions:

1. Heat 1 tbsp of oil over medium heat in a large pot and cook half the garlic for 1 to 2 minutes, until it starts to brown.

2. Add ¼ tsp of salt and the spinach and toss to combine it all. Cook for 3 to 5 minutes, stirring a couple of times until it is almost wilted. Take the pan off the heat, stir the lemon juice in, and transfer to a bowl. Cover to keep it warm.

3. Turn the heat up to medium-high, add the rest of the oil, and cook the remaining garlic for 1 to 2 minutes, until it starts to brown.

4. Add the cleaned shrimp, 1/8 tsp of salt, and the red pepper flakes. Cook, stirring frequently, for about 3 to 5 minutes, until the shrimp are just cooked.

5. Serve the shrimp on a bed of spinach and garnished with parsley and lemon zest.

Sheet-Pan Chicken with Roasted Spring Vegetables and Lemon Vinaigrette

Serves: 4

Ingredients:

- 2 boneless, skinless chicken breast halves (8 ounces each), sliced in half

- 2 cups of asparagus, chopped into 1-inch chunks

- 1 ½ cups of grape tomatoes, cut in half

- 1 ½ cups of cremini mushrooms, sliced

- ¼ cup of low-fat mayonnaise

- 6 minced garlic cloves

- 1 tbsp of olive oil

- ½ cup of panko breadcrumbs

- 3 tbsp of parmesan cheese, grated

- ½ tsp of black pepper

- ½ tsp of kosher salt

- Olive oil cooking spray

- Fresh dill for garnish

For the Vinaigrette:

- 1 whole lemon
- 1 tbsp of olive oil
- 1 tbsp of feta cheese, crumbled
- ½ tsp of honey

Instructions:

1. Preheat your oven to 475°F and place a large baking pan in it to heat up.

2. Make the vinaigrette. Grate the lemon and squeeze the juice. Mix 1 tbsp of juice with ½ tsp zest, and whisk in the olive oil, honey, and cheese. Set aside.

3. Wrap the chicken pieces in plastic wrap and flatten them using a meat mallet until they are ½-inch thick.

4. Put the chicken in a bowl, add 2 garlic cloves and the mayonnaise, and stir to combine.

5. Mix the parmesan, panko, ¼ tsp of pepper, and ¼ tsp of salt in a shallow dish, dip each chicken piece in it, coat it all over, and spray the top of each piece with a light squirt of cooking spray.

6. Place the mushrooms, asparagus, oil, tomatoes, and the rest of the garlic in a bowl. Add ¼ tsp each of salt and pepper and stir to combine.

7. Place the chicken at one end of the hot baking dish, add the vegetables on the other side, and bake for 18 to 20 minutes, until the veggies are tender and the chicken has an internal temperature of 165°F.

8. Serve with the vinaigrette drizzled over and garnished with dill.

Eggplant Parmesan

Serves: 6

Ingredients:

- 2 medium eggplant (about a lb. each)
- 2 large eggs
- 2 tbsp of water
- 1 cup of panko breadcrumbs
- ¾ cup of parmesan cheese, grated
- 1 tsp of Italian seasoning
- 1 jar of no-added-salt tomato sauce (24 ounces)
- ½ tsp of black pepper
- ½ tsp of salt
- ¼ cup of torn fresh basil leaves + extra for garnish
- 2 grated garlic cloves
- ½ tsp of crushed red pepper flakes
- 1 cup of part-skim mozzarella, shredded
- Olive oil or canola cooking spray

Instructions:

1. Preheat your oven to 400°F and place racks in the bottom and middle thirds. Spray a 9 x 13-inch baking dish and two baking trays with oil.

2. Slice the eggplants widthwise into ¼-inch thick slices.

3. Whisk the water and eggs together in a shallow dish and mix ¼ cup of grated parmesan, the breadcrumbs, and Italian seasoning in another one.

4. Dip each eggplant slice in the egg, then the breadcrumbs, coating all over and gently pressing them to ensure the crumbs stick.

5. Spray each side with cooking spray and layer them on the baking sheets in single layers.

6. Bake for 30 minutes until tender and just turning brown, turning the slices and switching the trays around halfway through cooking. Season with salt and pepper.

7. While the eggplant is cooking, mix the tomato sauce with the red pepper flakes and basil. Spread ½ a cup over the base of the prepared dish and layer half the cooked eggplant slices over the top. Smooth another cup of sauce over the top and add ½ a cup of mozzarella and ¼ cup of parmesan. Add the rest of the eggplant and the remaining sauce, and finish with the remaining cheese.

8. Bake for about 20 to 30 minutes, until the top is golden brown and the sauce is bubbling hot.

9. Leave it for 5 minutes to cool off and serve garnished with fresh basil.

Seared Scallops with White Bean Ragu and Charred Lemon

Serves: 4

Ingredients:

- 1 lb. of dry sea scallops, side muscle removed and discarded
- 1 can of rinsed and drained no-added-salt cannellini beans (15 ounces)
- 1 lb. of trimmed mature white chard or spinach, sliced thinly
- 3 tbsp of olive oil
- 2 minced garlic cloves
- 1 cup of low-salt chicken broth
- 1 tbsp of rinsed, chopped capers
- 1 tbsp of butter
- 2 tbsp of chopped fresh parsley
- 1 lemon, sliced in half
- ½ tsp of ground black pepper

Instructions:

1. Heat 2 tsp oil over medium-high heat in a large skillet and cook the greens for 4 minutes until wilted, stirring often. Add the capers, garlic, and ¼ tsp pepper. Cook for about 30 seconds until fragrant, stirring occasionally.

2. Add the broth, wine, and beans, bring it to a simmer, and turn the heat down. Cover the skillet and simmer

for 5 minutes before taking it off the heat and adding the butter. Stir it in, put the lid back on, and keep it warm.

3. Sprinkle the rest of the pepper over the scallops, and heat the rest of the oil over medium-high heat in a large pan. Cook the scallops for about 2 minutes on each side until browned all over.

4. Lift them onto a clean plate. Place the lemon halves, cut side down, in the pan and char them for about 2 minutes. Slice them into wedges.

5. Serve the bean ragu with the scallops and garnish with fresh parsley and lemon wedges.

Salmon and Asparagus with Lemon-Garlic Butter Sauce

Serves: 4

Ingredients:

- 1 lb. of center-cut wild salmon, cut into 4 equal pieces
- 1 lb. of trimmed fresh asparagus
- ½ tsp of salt
- ½ tsp of ground black pepper
- 3 tbsp of butter
- 1 tbsp of olive oil
- ½ tsp of grated fresh garlic
- 1 tbsp of lemon juice
- 1 tsp of lemon zest

Instructions:

1. Preheat your oven to 375°F and spray cooking spray over a large baking sheet.

2. Lay the salmon pieces on one half of the tray and place the asparagus on the other side. Season with salt and pepper.

3. Hea the garlic, oil, butter, lemon juice, and zest over medium heat in a small pan until the butter has completely melted. Drizzle it over the asparagus and salmon and bake for about 12 to 15 minutes, until the asparagus has just started to soften and the salmon is cooked through.

4. Serve hot.

Baked Halibut with Brussel Sprouts and Quinoa

Serves: 4

Ingredients:

- 1 lb. of trimmed, sliced Brussel sprouts
- 1 whole trimmed fennel bulb, sliced into strips
- 1 tbsp of olive oil + 1 tsp
- 1 lb. of halibut, sliced into 4 equal pieces
- 2 cups of cooked quinoa
- 2 tbsp of melted unsalted butter
- 3 tbsp of lemon juice
- 4 minced garlic cloves
- ¼ cup of sun-dried tomatoes, roughly chopped

- ¼ cup of pitted, chopped Kalamata olives
- 2 tbsp of fennel fronds or Italian parsley
- ½ tsp of salt
- ½ tsp of ground black pepper

Instructions:

1. Preheat your oven to 400°F and place racks in the top and middle thirds.
2. Place the sliced sprouts, fennel, ¼ tsp salt, ¼ tsp pepper, and 1 tbsp of oil in a bowl and toss to coat. Spread it over a large baking sheet and bake for 20 to 25 minutes until tender, stirring occasionally.
3. Place the halibut pieces on a separate large tray and top off with the rest of the salt and pepper and half the garlic. Mix the melted butter and lemon juice in a bowl and brush half of it over the halibut.
4. Bake for about 12 to 15 minutes until the fish is opaque and easy to flake with a fork.
5. Combine the cooked quinoa with the rest of the oil, the olives, tomatoes, and fennel or parsley fronds.
6. Stir the rest of the garlic into the lemon butter and pour it over the vegetables. Bake for a minute and serve hot with the halibut and quinoa.

Pistachio-Crusted Chicken with Warm Barley Salad

Serves: 4

Ingredients:

- 2 trimmed skinless, boneless chicken breasts, sliced in half widthwise (8 ounces each)
- 1 cup of shelled, salted pistachios
- 2 cups of water + 1 tbsp
- 1 cup of quick-cook barley
- ½ cup of whole wheat breadcrumbs
- 1 cup of halved cherry tomatoes
- 2 tbsp of olive oil
- 1 tbsp of white wine vinegar
- 1 egg white
- 1 cup of chopped fresh parsley
- 1 tsp of orange zest
- ½ tsp of salt
- ½ tsp of garlic powder
- Olive oil cooking spray

Instructions:

1. Preheat your oven to 450°F. Spray cooking spray over a wire rack and line a baking tray with aluminum foil.

2. Heat the barley and 2 cups of water in a small pan and bring it to a boil. Turn the heat down, cover the pan,

and simmer for 10 to 12 minutes until the barley is tender. Remove from the heat and set aside.

3. Place ¾ cup pistachios, the orange zest, breadcrumbs, and garlic powder in a food processor and chop coarsely. Place the mixture in a shallow dish.

4. Add the egg white and 1 tbsp of water in a bowl and whisk.

5. Wrap the chicken in plastic wrap and pound and to ½-inch thick. Sprinkle ¼ tsp of salt over the chicken, coat it in the egg mix, and then the pistachio mix, pressing it gently so the crumbs stick.

6. Place the chicken on the wire rack and spray with oil on both sides.

7. Bake for 15 minutes, until the internal temperature is 165°F.

8. Meanwhile, heat the oil over medium heat and cook the tomatoes and vinegar for about a minute until the tomatoes soften to the point of collapse. Take it off the heat.

9. Drain the barley, add it to the tomatoes, and add the rest of the pistachios, parsley, and salt. Stir well and serve hot with the chicken.

Beef Stir-Fry with Baby Bok Choy and Ginger

Serves: 4

Ingredients:

- 12 ounces of trimmed beef flank steak

- 1 lb. of trimmed baby Bok choy, sliced into 2-inch chunks

- 1 tbsp of fresh ginger, minced
- 1 ½ tbsp of low-salt soy sauce
- 1 tsp + 1 tbsp of dry sherry
- 1 tsp of cornstarch
- 1 tsp of toasted sesame oil
- 1 tbsp of vegetable oil
- 3 tbsp of salt-free chicken broth
- 2 tbsp of oyster sauce

Instructions:

1. Slice the beef along the grain into strips about 2 inches wide. Slice each piece across the grain into slices ¼-inch thick.

2. Place the beef, soy sauce, ginger, cornstarch, and 1 tsp sherry into a bowl and stir to dissolve the starch. Stir in the sesame oil, ensuring the beef is evenly coated.

3. Mix the rest of the sherry with the oyster sauce and set it aside.

4. Heat a large wok or skillet over high heat. Drop a little water in – if it vaporizes within a second or two, the pan is hot enough. Add the vegetable oil and swirl it around the pan to coat it. Place an even layer of beef in the pan and leave it to cook for about a minute until it starts to brown. Stir-fry it for up to a minute until brown all over but not completely cooked. Transfer the beef to a plate and set aside.

5. Add the broth and Bok choy to the pan and cover it. Cook for 1 to 2 minutes until the Bok choy is bright green and the liquid is almost all gone. Add the beef

back in and stir-fry for up to a minute until the Bok choy is crisp but tender and the beef is cooked through.

6. Serve hot.

Grilled Salmon and Vegetables

Serves: 4

Ingredients:

- 1 ¼ lb. of salmon fillet, sliced into 4 equal pieces
- 1 medium zucchini, cut in half lengthwise
- 2 bell peppers, trimmed, cut in half and deseeded
- 1 medium red onion, sliced into wedges of about 1 inch
- 1 tbsp of olive oil
- ½ tsp of salt
- ½ tsp of black pepper
- ¼ cup of fresh basil, sliced thinly
- 1 lemon, quartered

Instructions:

1. Preheat the grill to medium-high.

2. Brush oil over the peppers, zucchini, and onion, and sprinkle ¼ tsp salt over. Sprinkle the pepper and the rest of the salt over the salmon.

3. Place everything on the grill and cook the salmon for 8 to 10 minutes, or until flaky, and the vegetables for 4 to 6 minutes on each side, until they have grill marks on them and are just turning tender.

4. When the veggies have cooled enough to handle, chop them and place them in a large bowl. Toss together.

5. Slice the skin off the salmon and serve with the vegetables, garnished with fresh basil and lemon wedges.

Pan-Seared Steak with Crispy Herbs and Escarole

Serves: 4

Ingredients:

- 1 lb. of half-inch thick sirloin steak

- 16 cups of chopped escarole

- 2 tbsp of canola or grapeseed oil

- 4 crushed garlic cloves

- 5 fresh thyme sprigs

- 3 fresh sage sprigs

- 1 fresh rosemary sprig

- ½ tsp of salt

- ½ tsp of black pepper

Instructions:

1. Sprinkle ¼ tsp of slat and ¼ tsp of pepper over the steak.

2. Heat a large nonstick pan over medium-high heat and char the steak for 3 minutes on one side. Flip the steak, add the fresh herb sprigs, garlic, and oil, and cook for 3 to 4 minutes, stirring occasionally, until the meat is 125°F in the middle – check with a meat thermometer.

3. Place the steak on a plate, spoon the herbs and garlic over the top, and place a foil tent on it to keep it warm.

4. Cook the escarole seasoned with the rest of the salt and pepper for about 2 minutes, until the escarole is wilting, stirring frequently.

5. Slice the steak thinly and serve hot with the herbs and escarole.

Mexican Bake

Serves: 6

Ingredients:

- 1 ½ cups of cooked brown rice
- 1 lb. of boneless, skinless chicken breast chopped into small pieces
- 2 cans of crushed or diced no-added-salt tomatoes (14 ½ ounces each)
- 1 can of drained, rinsed, no-added-salt black beans (15 ounces)
- 1 cup of red bell pepper, chopped
- 1 cup of poblano pepper, chopped
- 1 cup of low-fat Monterey Jack cheese, shredded
- 1 cup of frozen corn kernels
- ¼ cup of sliced jalapeno pepper – OPTIONAL
- 1 tbsp of chili powder
- 1 tbsp of cumin
- 4 crushed garlic cloves

Instructions:

1. Preheat your oven to 400°F.

2. Spread the cooked rice in a 3-quart casserole dish and place the chicken pieces on top.

3. Mix the tomatoes, corn, beans, garlic, pepper, and seasonings and pour it over the chicken and rice.

4. Top with the jalapeno pepper slices and cheese, and bake for 45 minutes.

5. Serve hot.

DESSERTS AND SNACKS

The DASH diet is one of the few that doesn't restrict you from eating desserts, but you should limit yourself to no more than five, preferably fewer, portions per week and make them small. However, you can forget about having ice cream, as that is not allowed. Use yogurt or fruit in your desserts and ditch the added sugars; your sweet tooth will easily be satisfied.

Note that some recipes below include sugar, but the amount is lower than you think because they make several servings.

Easy Oat Milk Chocolate Pudding

Serves: 6

Ingredients:

- ¼ cup of granulated sugar
- ¼ cup of cocoa powder, unsweetened
- 2 tbsp of cornstarch
- 2 cups of oat milk, unsweetened
- 3 ounces of dark chocolate
- 1 tsp of vanilla extract
- 1/8 tsp of salt

Instructions:

1. Place the cocoa powder, sugar, salt, and cornstarch in a saucepan and whisk to combine.

2. Turn the heat to medium-high and gradually pour in the milk, whisking constantly, until you have a smooth,

chocolatey sauce. There must not be any lumps, or the final dessert will have lumps in it.

3. Continue heating and stirring for 10 minutes until the sauce bubbles and thickens. When your spoon is thickly coated without the mixture sliding off easily, add the chocolate and stir thoroughly until it has melted and the mixture is velvety smooth.

4. Remove the pan from the heat, add the vanilla, and continue stirring.

5. Chill or serve warm, garnished with fresh fruit if desired.

Blueberry Crumble Bars

Serves: 24

Ingredients:

- 3 ½ cups of steel cut or old-fashioned oats
- 2 ½ cups of almond meal, super-fine
- ½ cup of orange juice
- ½ cup of apple sauce, unsweetened
- 1/3 cup of organic maple syrup
- 2 tbsp of ground flaxseed
- 2 tsp of baking powder
- 2 tsp of cinnamon
- 1 ½ tsp of flaky sea salt
- 1 tsp of vanilla extract

For the Filling:

- 3 cups of fresh blueberries
- 1 tbsp of lemon juice
- 4 whole dates
- 3 tbsp of chia seeds
- 1 chopped nectarine – OPTIONAL

Instructions:

1. Preheat your oven to 350°F and line a 9 x 13 or 9 x 9-inch baking pan with parchment paper.

2. Place 2 cups of blueberries, the dates, and the lemon juice in a food processor and process. Scrape the sides of the bowl, process once more, and place the mixture in a small bowl. Add the chia seeds, stir to combine, and leave it on one side.

3. Wash the processor bowl, dry it, and add the almond meal, oats, baking powder, flaxseed, sea salt, and cinnamon. Pulse to mix it, and add the apple sauce, orange juice, maple syrup, and vanilla. Process to combine, scrape down the sides, and process once more. The mixture should be smooth and well mixed, a pasty batter.

4. Remove 1 ½ cups of the batter and set aside. Pour the rest into the baking pan and use your fingers or a spatula to smooth it into all four corners. Press it down to ensure it is firm in the pan. You can wet the spatula or your fingers to help make this easier.

5. Spread the blueberry mixture over the dough, sprinkle with the reserved cup of blueberries and the chopped nectarine if you are using it.

6. Spread the rest of the dough over the mixture evenly. It doesn't matter if it doesn't quite cover it completely, so long as it is even and smooth.

7. Bake for 40 minutes using the 9 x 9-inch pan or 30 minutes using the 9 x 13-inch tray. When the top is set and light brown, the crumble is done.

8. Remove the pan from the oven, let it cool, then slice it into bars or squares.

Chocolate Covered Chickpeas

Serves: 4

Ingredients:

- 1 cup of chickpeas
- 1 tbsp of avocado oil
- ½ cup of chocolate chips

Instructions:

1. Preheat your oven to 425°F and cover a baking tray with parchment paper.

2. Drain the chickpeas, rinse them, and shake them to get rid of any excess water.

3. Spread them out on paper towels, pat them dry, and pick off any loose skins. Spread the chickpeas over the lined baking tray and bake for 20 to 30 minutes until crispy.

4. Set them aside to cool.

5. Place parchment paper over another baking tray.

6. Put the chocolate chips in a small microwave-safe dish and heat until melted. Every 15 seconds, stir the

chocolate to stop it from burning. When it is almost melted, take the chocolate from the microwave, stir it, and add the avocado oil. Stir well, transfer to a larger bowl, and drop the chickpeas in.

7. Stir to coat thoroughly and transfer to the prepared tray. Lay them in a single layer, with a gap between them. Place the tray in the freezer for 15 minutes.

8. Once hardened, transfer to an airtight container and store in the refrigerator for up to 5 days.

Plum Oatmeal Crisp

Serves: 12

Ingredients:

For the Base:

- 30 plums
- Juice from a lemon
- 1/3 cup of sugar
- 3 tbsp of cornstarch – if the fruit is really juicy, use a little extra
- 1 tsp of ground cinnamon

For the Topping:

- 1 cup of old-fashioned oats
- ½ cup of all-purpose flour
- ½ packed cup of brown sugar
- 1/3 cup of margarine or butter
- ½ tsp of ground cinnamon

Instructions:

1. Preheat your oven to 350°F, and spray cooking spray over an 8 x 11-inch pan.

2. Wash the plums and drain them.

3. Dice them into bite-sized pieces and remove the pits. Put the plums in a large bowl and add the lemon juice. Stir to coat the plums and set aside.

4. Mix the sugar, cinnamon, and cornstarch in a small bowl and transfer it to the plums. Stir to combine and put the mixture into the prepared pan. Set to one side.

5. Make the topping. Combine the flour, oats, sugar, and cinnamon, and cut the butter in. Mix it all together to create a crumble mix.

6. Sprinkle it evenly over the plums and bake for 0 to 45 minutes until golden brown and bubbling hot.

7. Cool a little before you slice and serve it.

Strawberry Apple Crisp

Serves: 6

Ingredients:

For the Filling:

- 2 peeled, chopped medium apples
- 2 cups of sliced strawberries
- 2 tbsp of freshly squeezed lemon juice
- 1/3 cup of sugar
- 1/3 cup of all-purpose flour
- ½ tsp of vanilla extract

For the Topping:

- ½ packed cup + 1 packed tbsp of brown sugar
- ¼ cup of melted butter
- ½ cup of chopped walnuts
- ½ cup of chopped pecans
- ¾ cup of rolled oats
- 1 tsp of ground cinnamon
- ¼ tsp of nutmeg
- ¼ tsp of ground cloves
- 1/8 tsp of salt

Instructions:

1. Preheat your oven to 350°F and grease an 8 x 8-inch baking dish with a little butter.

2. Mix the strawberries, apples, vanilla, and lemon juice in a large bowl, ensuring the apples are coated in juice.

3. Add the flour and sugar, and stir to ensure the fruit is evenly coated.

4. Mix the butter, brown sugar, nutmeg, cinnamon, cloves, and salt in another large bowl, then add the oats and nuts and stir to combine.

5. Layer the fruit mixture over the bottom of the greased dish and top with the oat mixture.

6. Bake it until golden brown and bubbling hot, about 35 to 40 minutes. Remove it from the oven and leave it to cool down for 5 or 10 minutes before serving.

Strawberries with Peppered Balsamic Drizzle

Serves: 4 to 6

Ingredients:

- 1 quart rinsed, hulled, and sliced strawberries
- 3 tbsp of sugar
- 1 ½ tbsp of good-quality balsamic vinegar
- 1 tsp of black pepper

Instructions:

1. Place the berries in a glass bowl and sprinkle with the sugar.

2. Por the balsamic vinegar over, toss to coat, and set aside for 15 minutes so the strawberries can macerate in the vinegar.

3. After that, grind the pepper into the bowl, toss to coat, and leave for 5 minutes to allow the flavors to come out.

4. Leftovers can be chilled for up to 2 days or frozen. If you freeze them, their shape will go, but you can still use them as a sauce for other desserts.

Grilled Peaches with Honey, Yogurt, and Mint

Serves: 4

Ingredients:

- 2 large, fully ripe peaches
- 1 tbsp of soft brown sugar

- 5.3-ounce container of thick Greek or Skyr vanilla yogurt

- Organic honey

- 3 to 4 minced mint leaves

Instructions:

1. Slice each peach in half, carefully remove the pits, and sprinkle the cut sides with brown sugar.

2. Preheat the grill to low to medium-low heat and place the peaches cut-side down on the rack. Cook for about 8 minutes, until the peaches are starting to soften and warm. Turn them after about 4 minutes.

3. Lift the peaches from the grill, place them in serving dishes, and top with yogurt, a little honey, and mint.

Chocolate Covered Frozen Bananas

Serves: at least 2 dozen

Ingredients:

- 2 firm but ripe large bananas

- 12 ounces of chopped semi-sweet chocolate or dark chocolate chips

- 4 tbsp of refined, solid coconut oil

Instructions:

1. Slice each banana. Line a baking tray with wax or parchment paper and lay the banana slices on it. Freeze for about 2 hours until the slices are solid.

2. Place the chocolate in a microwave-safe bowl, add the coconut oil, and heat for 60 seconds. Stir until the chocolate is glossy and melted, heating for 15 seconds

if needed. Do NOT overheat it. Set it aside to cool a little.

3. Dip the banana slices into the chocolate, coating them all over. Allow the excess to drip off, then lay the slices back on the tray and freeze immediately.

4. Once completely frozen, transfer them to a Ziploc bag or freezer-safe container for storage until you want them. Eat within 7 days.

Apricot-Sunflower Granola Bars

Serves: 24

Ingredients:

- 3 cups of old-fashioned oats
- 1 cup of dried apricots, finely chopped
- 1 cup of brown crispy rice cereal
- ½ cup of toasted unsalted pepitas
- ½ cup of toasted unsalted sunflower seeds
- ¼ tsp of salt
- 2/3 cup of light corn or brown rice syrup
- ½ cup of sunflower seed butter
- 1 tsp of ground cinnamon

Instructions:

1. Preheat your oven to 325°F and place parchment paper in a 9 x 13-inch baking tin, allowing the parchment paper to hang over two dies of the pan. Spray it with a light coat of cooking spray and set aside.

2. Place the oats, apricots, cereal, sunflower seeds, pepitas, and salt in a bowl and stir to combine.

3. Put the syrup, butter, and cinnamon into a microwave-safe dish and cook for 30 seconds. Stir and pour it into the dry ingredients, stirring until everything is combined. Place it into the baking pan and press it firmly down into the pan with a spatula.

4. Bake for 20 to 25 minutes for chewy bars until the bars are soft in the center, and the edges start changing color. If you want crunchy bars, bake for 30 to 35 minutes.

5. Allow the pan to cool for 10 minutes, then lift the mixture out using the parchment paper. Slice it into 24 even pieces, but don't separate them. Cool for 30 minutes, then separate and store for up to 1 week.

Cherry-Cocoa-Pistachio Energy Balls

Serve: 32 balls

Ingredients:

- 1 ½ cups of dried cherries
- ¾ cup of salted pistachios shelled
- ½ cup of almond butter
- 3 tbsp of unsweetened cocoa powder
- 4 tbsp of organic maple syrup
- ½ tsp of cinnamon

Instructions:

1. Put all the ingredients in a food processor and finely chop them, pulsing 10 to 20 times for a minute. Scrape

the sides down as needed. The mixture should be crumbly but can be formed into a ball.

2. Wet your hands and roll 1 tbsp of mixture into a ball. Repeat until all the mixture is used and refrigerate for up to a week in an airtight container, or freeze for no more than 3 months.

Air-Fryer Sweet Potato Chips

Serves: 8

Ingredients:

- 1 sweet potato, sliced into rounds about 1/8th-inch thick
- 1 tbsp of canola oil
- ¼ tsp of ground black pepper
- ¼ tsp of salt

Instructions:

1. Soak the potato slices in cold water for 20 minutes, then drain and use paper towels to pat them dry.

2. Dry the bowl and put the potato slices back in it. Add the oil, pepper, and salt and toss to coat.

3. Spray cooking spray over an air fryer basket and place a single layer of potato slices in it. Cook at 350°F for 15 minutes until crispy and cooked, flipping them at every 5-minute mark and keeping them in a single layer.

4. Transfer them to a plate and repeat until all the slices are cooked.

5. Allow them to cool down for 5 minutes and then serve, or cool them completely and store them for up to 3 days in an airtight container.

Kale Chips

Serves: 4

Ingredients:

- 1 large bunch of destemmed and torn kale
- 1 tbsp of olive oil
- ¼ tsp of salt

Instructions:

1. Preheat your oven to 400°F and place racks in the middle and upper thirds.

2. Dry the kale as much as possible with paper towels and place it in a large bowl.

3. Drizzle with the oil, sprinkle the salt over, and massage it to coat the kale with your clean hands.

4. Layer the kale on 2 large baking trays, ensuring they do not overlap. If necessary, do this in batches.

5. Bake for about 8 to 12 minutes, until the leaves are crispy. Halfway through, change the pans around to make sure they cook evenly. If you are only using one tray, check at 8 minutes – you don't want them to burn.

6. Allow them to cool a little and serve or store in an airtight container for no more than a day or two.

Chapter 6: Adapting the DASH Diet to Different Lifestyles

The DASH diet is one of the easiest to adapt, regardless of your lifestyle. While it contains meat and fish, switching those out is easy if you follow a vegan or vegetarian lifestyle. If you are busy, don't worry. Many DASH diet recipes are simple to prepare, and you can even prepare many of them ahead of time and fill your freezer with delicious, easy meals that just need reheating.

Let's dive into adapting this diet to match your lifestyle.

12. DASH dieting can be applied to vegan and vegetarian lifestyles too! Source: https://pixabay.com/photos/sandwich-vegetarian-sandwich-1051605/

DASH Diet for Vegans and Vegetarians

The DASH diet is easy to adapt if you follow a vegetarian or vegan lifestyle, as there is a strong emphasis on fruit, vegetables, whole grains, healthy fats (plenty of these come from a plant-based source), and lean protein.

One of the best aspects of DASH is that there are plenty of foods to choose from, and what you can eat far outweighs what you can't. All these foods can easily be found in farmer's markets and grocery stores. How much you eat is dependent on your calorie requirements per day. The food list below is for an 1800-calorie-per-day diet:

Fruit: 4 to 5 servings per day. One serving is ¼ cup of dried fruit, a medium piece of whole raw fruit, ½ cup of frozen or fresh fruit, or ½ cup of pure fruit juice (100%). Virtually all fruits are allowed on the diet, including:

- Apples
- Apricots
- Bananas
- Blackberries
- Blueberries
- Grape
- Grapefruit
- Mango
- Oranges
- Peaches
- Pineapples

- Raspberries

- Strawberries

- Tangerines

- Watermelon

And many more besides. That includes frozen, fresh, and dried fruit, and the best dried fruits to eat are raisins, prunes, figs, and dates.

Vegetables: 4 to 5 servings per day. One serving is ½ cup of cooked or raw vegetables, 1 cup of leafy greens (raw), or ½ cup of pure vegetable juice. There are no restrictions on what vegetables you can eat, and the best options include:

- Bell peppers

- Broccoli

- Cauliflower

- Collard greens

- Green beans

- Kale

- Peas

- Spicy peppers

- Spinach

- Summer squash

- Sweet potato

- Tomato

- Winter squash

- Zucchini

Grains: 6 servings per day. The best grains are:

- Amaranth
- Brown rice
- Buckwheat
- Bulgur
- Oats
- Quinoa
- Teff
- Wholegrain bread
- Wholewheat bread
- Wild rice

Nuts, Seeds, and Legumes: 4 servings per week. One serving is 2 tbsp of seed or nut butter, 1/3 cup of nuts, or ½ cup of cooked legumes. Choose from any you want, the best options being:

- Cannellini beans
- Chickpeas
- Garbanzo beans
- Kidney beans
- Lentils
- Navy beans

Healthy Fats: 2 to 3 servings daily. One serving is 1 tsp of oil, such as coconut, avocado, canola, or olive oil. Other great sources of good fat are almond butter, no-sugar natural peanut butter, and whole avocadoes.

Sample Vegetarian/Vegan DASH Diet Menu

This is what a DASH diet menu might look like for vegans or vegetarians:

DAY ONE:

- **Breakfast**: Plain coconut milk with berries and walnuts.

- **Lunch**: Greek salad.

- **Dinner**: Three-bean and tomato chili.

DAY TWO:

- **Breakfast**: Steel-cut oatmeal with banana and peanut butter.

- **Lunch**: Pita with veggies and hummus.

- **Dinner**: Lentils with kale and brown rice.

DAY THREE:

- **Breakfast**: One slice of gluten-free toast with veggie and chickpea scramble and an orange.

- **Lunch**: Vegetable and black bean wrap.

- **Dinner**: Wholegrain, gluten-free pasta with fresh tomato sauce and a spinach side salad.

DASH Diet for a Busy Lifestyle

Finding the time to eat a healthy diet isn't easy when your schedule is non-stop hectic. That sort of lifestyle plus the added stress of trying to fit in a good meal leads to your body releasing stress hormones – adrenaline (norepinephrine) and noradrenaline (cortisol) – which can significantly affect your food choices. When stressed, you might eat more sweet, fatty, and salty foods, which trigger feel-good hormones to be released into your bloodstream. However, that buzz is inevitably followed by a crash, leading to you feeling stressed and miserable again, so the cycle continues. It doesn't have to be that way. The following strategies can help you fit the DASH diet into your busy lifestyle easily and with the minimum amount of fuss:

- **Meal Prep**: When you plan and prep your meals ahead of time, weekday mealtimes become a breeze. Set aside some time at the weekend to batch-cook soups, stews, and casseroles. If you can find the time in the evening, prep a crockpot meal for the following day – start cooking it when you go to work and dinner will be ready when you get home. Prepare easy snacks and bag them up, like cut veggies, grapes, etc.

- **Eat Whole Foods**: They are packed with vitamins, minerals, and fiber, far more than processed foods. Purchase pre-packed salads, pre-cut veggies and fruit, and easy-to-eat fruits – apples, bananas, oranges, etc.

- **Have a Good Breakfast**: Starting the day with a good meal helps steady your blood sugar levels, so have a breakfast with a good balance of protein, fiber, carbs, and fat. The carbs will give you energy, the protein keeps you going, and fat and fiber keep you full for longer, so you won't be tempted to snack.

- **Make Protein Your Priority**: Protein fills you up and slows the speed at which sugar is released into the blood. Eat lean meat, fish, chicken, nuts, grains, seeds, and lentils.

- **Get Some Exercise**: You don't have to find the time to do a full half-hour workout every morning. Ten minutes, three times a day, is good enough, or build it into your day – get off the bus a stop earlier, take the stairs, go for a quick walk at lunchtime, and so on.

- **Remember Why**: Knowing your reason for changing your diet is the best way to keep yourself motivated. Write your reason down where you can see it, and look at it when you feel your motivation slipping.

Family-Friendly DASH Diet Recipes

It isn't always easy to cook when you have kids underfoot, and it's even worse if they are picky eaters. Luckily, the DASH diet offers some family-friendly recipes that are sure to delight your kids and are easy to prepare:

Strawberry Waffles

Ingredients:

- 1 cup of all-purpose flour
- 2 tsp of baking powder
- 1 tbsp of sugar
- 1 whole egg
- 1 cup of milk
- 2 tbsp of vegetable oil or melted butter
- ½ cup of diced strawberries
- ¼ tsp of salt

Instructions:

1. Set up a mini waffle maker to heat.
2. Whisk the sugar, flour, salt, and baking powder in one bowl and the egg, butter/oil, and milk in another.

3. Add the wet to the dry ingredients, whisking gently, and fold the strawberries in.

4. Add ¼ cup of batter to the waffle maker, cook until golden brown, and set aside. Repeat with the rest of the batter.

Air Fryer Sweet Potato Fries

Ingredients:

- 2 peeled sweet potatoes cut into 14-inch fries
- ¼ tsp of kosher salt
- ¼ tsp of cornstarch

Instructions:

1. Soak the fries in cold water for 30 minutes, then drain and pat with paper towels.

2. Put them in a dry bowl, add the cornstarch, and toss to coat.

3. Place a single layer of fries in the air fryer and cook for 10 minutes at 350°F. Give the fries a shake, turn the heat to 400°F, and cook for 5 minutes.

4. Remove, toss in salt and serve.

Air Fryer Burgers

Ingredients:

- 1 lb. of 90% lean ground beef
- 1 whole egg
- 2 tsp of kosher salt
- ¼ cup of breadcrumbs

- ½ tsp of onion powder
- ½ tsp of garlic powder
- ½ tsp of black pepper
- ½ tsp of smoked paprika
- ½ tsp of Worcestershire sauce

Instructions:

1. Place all the ingredients in a bowl and combine them using your hands.

2. For it into patties, approximately 4 to 5 inches. Place two patties in the air fryer and cook for 10 minutes at 375°F or until done to your desire.

3. Serve with wholewheat buns.

Candied Brussel Sprouts

Ingredients:

- 1 lb. of Brussels sprouts
- 2 ounces of partly cooked thick-cut bacon
- 2 tbsp of organic maple syrup
- 1 tbsp of olive oil
- 1 tsp of sea salt

Instructions:

1. Trim the sprouts, remove the loose leaves, and slice them in half. Slice the bacon into ½-inch chunks.

2. Put the oil, syrup, and salt in a bowl, add the sprouts, and toss to coat.

3. Cook in the air fryer for 8 to 10 minutes at 400°F. Serve hot.

Potato Pancakes

Ingredients:

- 2 peeled medium potatoes
- ½ yellow onion
- 1 whole egg
- 2 tbsp of wholewheat flour
- ½ tsp of salt
- ½ tsp of onion powder
- ¼ tsp of black pepper

Instructions:

1. Grate the potatoes and onion.
2. Put the rest of the ingredients in a bowl, add the onion and potato, and combine.
3. Form into small patties and fry in a little hot oil until cooked through, a few minutes on each side.
4. Serve with applesauce and non-fat yogurt.

Air Fryer Mac N Cheese Balls

Ingredients:

- 4 cups of elbow macaroni, cooked
- 3 cups of fine breadcrumbs
- 3 whole eggs
- 4 tbsp of vegetable or grapeseed oil

- 2 tbsp of chopped fresh parsley
- 1 tbsp of butter
- 1 cup + 3 tsp of flour
- 1 1/3 cups of heavy cream
- 2 cups of shredded Monterey Jack cheese
- 2 cups of shredded sharp cheddar cheese
- 4 dashes of hot sauce
- 2 tsp of sea salt
- ½ tsp of garlic granules
- ¼ tsp of smoked paprika
- ¼ tsp of black pepper

Instructions:

1. Heat the butter over medium heat and whisk 1 cup of flour in for 1 minute.

2. Add the cream, whisk, and heat. Whisk in 1 ½ cups each of the cheddar and Monterey Jack cheeses when it is hot. Do this gradually and keep whisking until the cheese has melted.

3. Add the paprika, salt, garlic, hot sauce, and pepper and whisk to combine.

4. Add the cooked pasta and stir to combine. Take the pan off the heat, add the rest of the cheese and parsley, and fold it in.

5. Line a tray with parchment paper and transfer the macaroni cheese to it. Refrigerate for 30 minutes.

6. Combine the oil and breadcrumbs and preheat the air fryer to 360°F.

7. Form the cooled mixture into 2-inch balls and dredge them in the remaining flour. Beat the eggs, dip the balls in, and then in the breadcrumbs.

8. Air fry them in single layers, no more than 8 balls at a time, for 12 minutes, shaking gently halfway through cooking. Repeat with the rest and eat immediately or store in an airtight container.

Gluten-Free Chocolate Chip Cookies

Ingredients:

- 1 cup of smooth almond butter
- 2/3 cup of muscovado sugar
- 1 whole egg
- 1 tsp of vanilla extract
- 1/3 cup of small chocolate chips
- ½ tsp of almond extract
- ½ tsp of baking soda

Instructions:

1. Blend the butter and sugar using an electric hand mixer. Beat the egg and mix it into the butter. Add the baking soda, vanilla, and almond, and blend to a smooth consistency.

2. Stir in the chocolate chips and form the mixture into small balls about the size of a teaspoon.

3. Press them into cookies and air fry for 6 to 8 minutes at 350°F, until the edges are turning golden brown. Leave to cool before eating.

Chapter 7: Tips for Sustaining a DASH Lifestyle

Starting a diet is one thing, but sustaining it is something else entirely. Life gets in the way, and sometimes, all your good intentions go out the window. This chapter will discuss how you can overcome challenges that get in the way, how to keep your motivation going, and look at some of the long-term, proven benefits of the DASH diet.

13. Sustaining a healthy diet can be challenging, but nothing that you cannot overcome. Source: https://pixabay.com/photos/tray-breakfast-muesli-fruits-bowls-2546077/

Overcoming Challenges and Maintaining Your Motivation

It's thrilling, isn't it? You've decided you need to change your diet, planned your meals, done your shopping, and even prepped some meals for the weeks ahead to make life easier. Things will go as planned for a week, maybe a month, but then something happens, and you slide off the wagon.

Roadblocks are nothing new. They happen in any diet or lifestyle, and the biggest challenge is learning to face and overcome them so you can continue your good work. Perhaps the biggest challenge most people face is changing how and what they eat. It's difficult to do, especially if you are used to eating a diet of junk and processed food. The DASH diet is focused mostly on healthy, whole foods, a completely different way of eating for most people, and the urge to eat what you consider "normal" food will be high for a while.

Planning and prepping are the easiest ways to overcome these urges and ensure that you don't have those "normal" foods in the house. Fill your fridge and freezer with healthy meals and snacks, and you'll be more likely to stick to your diet. Experiment with the recipes, too. Change up the ingredients, make them so they suit you, so long as you stick to the principles of the DASH diet.

Make sure you include a varied range of foods in your diet. Variety is the spice of life, and it makes meal times more interesting. You'll note that the 30-day sample meal plan included in this guide has completely different meals every day – no repeats. Many diets advocate eating the same thing several times a week to make it easy. Yes, you can do that if it suits you, but you'll get bored soon.

What about socializing? You don't want to miss the chance of having a meal out with friends because the food might not fit your diet. Most restaurants provide their menus online, so find it, go through it, and work out what you can eat. Contact the restaurant and ask if they can change up some ingredients to suit your diet. Most will accommodate customers if they can, provided they get enough notice.

Perhaps the most important thing is to be kind to yourself, especially in the early days. Keep your family and friends in the loop, as they can support you, making those important social occasions even more enjoyable. You will occasionally slip up, but you mustn't beat yourself up. Get straight back on the horse and set off again. One slip-up won't do any damage – the damage is done if you keep slipping up and gradually slide back into your old ways.

Proven Benefits

The DASH diet is one of the most researched diets in the world, and that's good news. It means there is plenty of evidence showing the long-term benefits of this science-backed diet:

14. Researchers found plenty of benefits to DASH dieting. Source: https://pixabay.com/photos/engineer-sports-engineering-office-4922798/

- **It Lowers Blood Pressure:** Within 14 days of starting the diet, your blood pressure will be reduced by a few points. Keep it up, and you could see an 8 to 14-point drop over the long term.

- **Prevents Osteoporosis:** The diet strengthens your bones and stops osteoporosis because your calcium intake is significantly increased from low-fat dairy and leafy greens.

- **Lower Cancer Risk:** Eating a diet rich in fruits and veggies and ditching processed food lowers your risk of cancer over the long term.

- **Reduced Risk of Metabolic Disorders:** This includes diabetes and cardiovascular disease, and it's because your food intake is balanced, lower in fat, sugar, and salt, and replacing simple sugars with complex carbohydrates. This reduces your LDL and total cholesterol while reducing blood pressure at the same time.

Unlike many fad diets, the DASH diet is solid. It isn't a fad, it doesn't deprive you, and it offers complete nutrition, not to mention helping you establish the habit of long-term healthy eating.

Relevant Trials

Perhaps one of the forerunners in DASH diet trials, the NHLBI (National Heart, Lung, and Blood Institute) has carried out several trials over the last 30+ years, seeking to discover if changes to diet really can help lower blood pressure. Here's what they found.

- **The DASH Trial:** This involved 459 people with a mixture of high and normal blood pressure, and three diets were compared, each having a daily sodium amount of 3000 mg: standard American diet, standard with extra veggies and fruits, and the DASH diet. All food and drink were provided, and after 8 weeks, those on the DASH diet and the standard with more veggies and fruit had reduced their blood pressure, the DASH participants showing the greatest reductions.

- **The DASH-Sodium Trial:** This involved 412 adults, some on DASH, some on a standard American diet. All food and drinks were provided for 4 weeks. The participants were a mixture of different sodium intakes: 3300 mg, 2300 mg, and 1500 mg. The trial concluded that a lower sodium intake led to lower blood pressure. However, the DASH-Low Sodium participants had much greater reductions than anyone else.

- **The OmniHeart Trial:** This trial included 164 adults with systolic BP of 120 to 159 mmHg and diastolic BP of 80 to 99 mmHg. Three diets were compared, each with a 2300 mg sodium intake: DASH, DASH with 10% of daily carb calories swapped for protein calories, and 10 of carb calories swapped for unsaturated fat calories. All food and drinks were provided for 6 weeks. The participants had a gap of 2 to 4 weeks between each diet when they ate their normal diet. The results showed no change in body weight, but the modified DASH diets showed a much better reduction in blood pressure and increase in lipid levels than the standard DASH diet and a much lower risk of heart disease.

- **The OmniCarb Trial:** This trial included 163 obese or overweight people with systolic BP of 120 to 159 mmHg and diastolic BP of 80 to 99 mmHg. Four DASH-like diets were compared, each with a 2300 mg daily sodium intake: high carb DASH with high GI (glycemic index), high carb DASH with low GI, low carb DASH with high GI, and low carb DASH with low GI. All food and drinks were provided for 5 weeks, and between diets, the participants had a gap of 2 weeks eating their own diet. Bodyweight did not change, and the low GI diets did not improve cholesterol, blood pressure, or insulin resistance, whereas the high GI diets did. This showed that using the index to choose foods for a DASH diet does not necessarily improve health.

- **The PREMIER Clinical Trial**: 810 participants took part in this trial, all with systolic B of 120 to 159 mmHg and diastolic BP of 80 to 95 mmHg. They were divided into three groups, each on a different program to reduce weight and blood pressure and improve their health over 6 months: advice-only with no behavioral change counseling, an established program with counseling, and an established program with counseling and the DASH diet. Participants were expected to provide their own food and drinks in this case. After 6 months, all three groups saw a reduction in blood pressure. The two groups where counseling was included lost more weight than the first group but the third group who followed the DASH diet showed the greatest blood pressure reductions.

These are just some of the studies, but all show that the DASH diet successfully reduces blood pressure, improves lipids, can result in some weight loss, and cuts the risk of certain diseases. They all agree – that less sodium in the diet is healthier and reduces the risk of heart disease, stroke, diabetes, and other health conditions.

Chapter 8: Resources and Further Reading

You've reached the end of this guide and it's hoped that you found it useful. However, this is only a basic guide, and plenty more information can be found on the DASH diet, including many other books and research papers. To finish, here is a list of other resources you can use to get more information about the diet and make an informed decision on whether it is right for you. Of course, you should consult your doctor or other healthcare provider to ensure the DASH diet suits you, especially if you have a health condition and are already taking medication.

15. There is plenty of information that can be found on the DASH diet. Source: https://pixabay.com/photos/books-bookstore-book-reading-1204029/

Cookbooks

The DASH Diet Mediterranean Solution: The Best Eating Plan to Control Your Weight and Improve Your Health for Life (A DASH Diet Book) by Marla Heller

Dash Diet Cookbook for beginners: The ultimate guide to managing blood pressure problems, with lots of low-sodium recipes and an 8-week meal plan. By Grace Ruiz

DASH Diet Meal Prep: 100 Healthy Recipes and 6 Weekly Plans by Maria-Paula Carrillo MS RDN LD, Katie McKee MCN RDN LD

DASH Diet For Dummies by Sarah Samaan, Rosanne Rust, Cindy Kleckner

DASH Diet Food List: The World's Most Comprehensive DASH Diet Ingredient List - Take It Wherever You Go! (Food Heroes) by Dash Heroes

The Mediterranean DASH Diet Cookbook: Lower Your Blood Pressure and Improve Your Health by Abbie Gellman RD MS CDN

The DASH Diet Weight Loss Blueprint: How to Lower Your Blood Pressure Naturally While Losing Inches off Your Waist by Elaine Summers

References

Dash Diet to Stop Hypertension

Harvard T H Chan School of Public Health: DASH Diet Review

Mayo Clinic: Nutrition and Healthy Eating

The Association of Dietary Approaches to Stop Hypertension (DASH) Diet with the Risk of Colorectal Cancer: A Meta-Analysis of Observational Studies

DASH Eating Plan

Online Communities and Resources

Mediterranean DASH Diet Support Group

DASH Diet for High Blood Pressure and Weight Loss Group

Dashdiet.org

Conclusion

Thank you for reading *"Dash Diet Cookbook for Beginners: An Easy-to-Follow Guide with Delicious Low Sodium Recipes and a 30-Day Meal Plan for a Sustainable Lifestyle."* Hopefully, you found it helpful, and it's given you everything you need to change your diet and lifestyle.

In this guide, you learned a lot of information about the DASH diet. In Chapter 1, you learned what the DASH diet is and how it can benefit you. In Chapter 2, you got an overview of sodium, why a certain level of it is important but too much is bad for you, while Chapter 3 talked about getting started with DASH. This included setting your goals and expectations ahead of time, making it easier for you to start and stick to your new lifestyle.

Chapter 4 gave you a sample 30-day meal plan, an idea of what you can eat every day, showing you that the diet is not hard and offers up delicious, fulfilling foods for the whole family.

Chapter 5 gave you all the recipes in the plan, plus some extras to help you make the diet work for you. In Chapter 6, you learned how to adapt the DASH diet to your lifestyle, including how to make it work if you follow a vegan or vegetarian diet or if you think you are too busy to even think about changing your diet.

Chapter 7 gave you some tips on sustaining your new lifestyle, including how to deal with challenges that arise and how to keep your motivation going, while Chapter 8 provided you with plenty of extra resources to get more information about the DASH diet.

Health is important, and while doctors are happy to hand out medication for just about anything these days, not everything needs to be fixed by pills. Simple changes to your diet and lifestyle can make a world of difference, and that's why the DASH diet is so easy to follow – it is easy to follow, and the whole family will enjoy and benefit from it.

If you enjoyed this book, please consider leaving a review on Amazon.

References

American Heart Association. (2018, April 16). 9 Grocery Shopping Tips. Heart. https://www.heart.org/en/healthy-living/healthy-eating/cooking-skills/shopping/grocery-shopping-tips

Beiser, A. (2023, September 11). The 30 BEST DASH Diet Recipes. Gypsy Plate. https://gypsyplate.com/the-best-dash-diet-recipes/

Better Health. (n.d.). Salt | betterhealth.vic.gov.au. Better Health. https://www.betterhealth.vic.gov.au/health/healthyliving/salt#high-sodium-intake-and-blood-pressure

Braun, A. (2021, September 2). Setting S.M.A.R.T. Goals for Weight Loss. Ro. https://ro.co/weight-loss/smart-goals-weight-loss/

Briskin, L. (2022, July 18). 7-Day DASH diet meal plan. Live Science. https://www.livescience.com/dash-diet-meal-plan

Cloyd, J. (2022, December 16). 9 Health Benefits of the DASH Diet. Rupa Health. https://www.rupahealth.com/post/9-health-benefits-of-the-dash-diet

Eat Good Feel Good. (2020, March 25). Our Favorite Kid-Friendly Recipes. Dash. https://bydash.com/blogs/eatgoodfeelgood/kid-friendly-recipes

Founder, D. E. G. (2018, November 28). DASH Diet: A Plant-Based Meal Plan for Heart Health. Dr. Group's Healthy Living Articles. https://explore.globalhealing.com/dash-diet/

Harvard School of Public Health. (2019, May 7). Salt and Sodium. The Nutrition Source. https://www.hsph.harvard.edu/nutritionsource/salt-and-sodium/

Heller, M. (2020). What Is the DASH Diet? Dash Diet. https://dashdiet.org/what-is-the-dash-diet.html

Jurek, P. (2022, February 15). 6 Strategies For Losing Weight When You Have A Busy Schedule. Henry Ford. https://www.henryford.com/blog/2022/02/losing-weight-with-a-busy-schedule

Nutrition, C. for F. S. and A. (2021). Sodium in Your Diet. FDA. https://www.fda.gov/food/nutrition-education-resources-materials/sodium-your-diet#:~:text=The%20words%20%E2%80%9Ctable%20salt%E2%80%9D%20and

Rosenbloom, C. (2022, August 29). 7-Day DASH Diet Meal Plan & Recipe Prep. Verywell Fit. https://www.verywellfit.com/7-day-dash-diet-meal-plan-and-recipe-prep-6374399

Seaver, V. (2024, January 12). 7-Day DASH Diet Menu. EatingWell. https://www.eatingwell.com/article/289964/7-day-dash-diet-menu/

The Heart Dietitian: Your Expert in Heart Healthy Eating -. (2022, February 17). The Heart Dietitian. https://theheartdietitian.com/

Thomas, L. (2018, May 23). DASH Diet Health Benefits. News Medical . https://www.news-medical.net/health/DASH-Diet-Health-Benefits.aspx

West, H. (2018, October 17). The DASH Diet: A Complete Overview and Meal Plan. Healthline. https://www.healthline.com/nutrition/dash-diet#foods-to-eat

Printed in Great Britain
by Amazon

40042600R00109